"Natalie Runion puts her finger dire[ct] ..... church with very practical counsel for how to realign God's houses of worship with the original purpose of the Church. A powerful word with a very practical plan."

Jentezen Franklin, senior pastor of Free Chapel and *New York Times* bestselling author

"Like the Christian life, the Church is held to a seemingly impossible standard: perfection. Because our standard is Jesus, we continuously fall short both in our daily lives and in our collective Church life. But Natalie has found the courageous option of not giving up on the Church and is sounding the alarm for us to wake up and restore the house that Jesus built!"

Marcus Mecum, lead pastor of 7 Hills Church

"With piercing imagery, bold conviction, and inspiring humility, my friend Natalie challenges leaders to build people instead of platforms, and sheep to search for shepherds instead of celebrities. This book serves as an exegetical blueprint of what Jesus had in mind when he said, 'My house shall be called a house of prayer.'"

Brandon Cormier, lead pastor of Zeal Church, Colorado Springs

"Let me applaud you, Natalie, for being so brave to address issues in the Church at large. However, let me throw confetti all over you for doing it with such grace and love! No church is perfect. No church leader is perfect. The 'church,' and we as leaders, have wounded and hurt so many people, and for that I'm so sad. My prayer is that I, along with the Natalies of the world, can lovingly ask the questions and be a part of the answers to lead like Jesus wants us to lead. Let's *all* be a part of the answer!"

Hope Carpenter, cofounder and pastor of Redemption Church, speaker, author, podcaster, wife, mom of three, GiGi to five

"What a needed book for our generation and for those coming after us! For a few decades we have experienced various expressions of the Body of Christ around the globe. And we have found that, although she is flawed, the Church is beautiful and still God's answer for the world! *The House That Jesus Built* is a timely reminder of the blueprint God has established in Scripture for the Church's construction. May we return to that blueprint and build God's way."

David and Nicole Binion, songwriters,
worship recording artists, and senior pastors
of Dwell Church in Dallas, Texas

"We are in the transition of a great change so we don't stay in the rut that kills the move of the Spirit and reduces the Church to religious drones. But while great change seems tumultuous and radical, these are actually days of beautiful revolution as God breathes upon a remnant called to lead the Church back to her first love and his original plan. Natalie Runion is one of those bridge builders standing at the dawn of a new day gently and passionately leading the Church into her finest hour, and this book is the very manual that will help them lay down their chains and step into it."

Nate Johnston, prophetic voice and
author of *The Wild Ones*

"From survival to revival, Natalie's newest book will save churches from the death spiral and set them on fire with a genuine move of the Holy Spirit. Natalie is surprisingly transparent, straightforward, fair, and redemptive. One of the best books on leading and being a healthy church."

Jerry and Kimberly Dirmann, lead pastors of The
Rock Campuses and Jesus Way Home Churches

"A prophetic and timely word for the era of church history in which we find ourselves. Readers' hearts will burn with equal parts pain and hope. This message is for the 'right now' remnant who will commit to rebuild from the ruins with Jesus. Every church leader should read this book."

Gunter Akridge, lead pastor of The Dwelling Church,
Savannah, Georgia, and author of *Kill the Dragon*

"Natalie doesn't merely 'call out,' she calls us up. *The House That Jesus Built* is a prophetic picture of what could be in the modern church—a healthy (not perfect) community that hosts the Holy Spirit's presence, shares life together, and perhaps above all, acts as a supernatural witness of the 'age to come' in the here and now. Get ready to be stirred: I dare say, this book can be a blueprint to stewarding sustained revival in our day."

Larry Sparks, MDiv, publisher for Destiny
Image and author of *Pentecostal Fire*

"Natalie has done it again! A book that hits home for those of us in the church community. It is a call to examine ourselves and our motives to make sure that we are aligned with a biblical model of God's Church, not the popular culture or old religious traditions. Every pastor and church leader should read this, allowing the Holy Spirit to speak his truth into our lives and our churches."

Shelly Swann, senior pastor of Faith Church Lubbock

"With every sentence, I was drawn in by the passion that Natalie penned, fueled by her love for Jesus and his Church. She is an excellent storyteller, possessing a solid biblical understanding of what the Church could and should be. Natalie isn't afraid to call church leaders to be true shepherds and invite those who have been wounded to embrace the hopeful vision of the Church that Jesus imparted to his disciples. I am deeply thankful for Natalie's voice in this pivotal moment for the Church."

David Ruybalid, religious trauma-informed coach and
associate pastor at Life Church Peoria, Peoria, Arizona

"Just like with *Raised to Stay*, Natalie in *The House That Jesus Built* isn't afraid to address issues that are considered taboo and often pushed aside. God is using her to be the voice for those who have been silenced. This book is a must-read not only for those in ministry but for all Christians. In the world we live in, we must be willing to hold ourselves accountable and learn how to truly live in the house that Jesus built."

Andrew Sapp, creative arts pastor of Metropolitan Church, Birmingham, Alabama

"In *The House That Jesus Built*, Natalie acutely diagnoses the problems and pain in the modern church, not as a divisive outsider throwing stones, but as a daughter of the house who longs that we return to building on the one true and solid foundation, Jesus Christ. This book is a prophetic blueprint urging us to partner with God in building his glorious Kingdom instead of our own little man-made castles."

Craig Cooney, lead pastor of HOPE Church, Northern Ireland, author of *The Tension of Transition* and *The Blueprint*, and founder of Daily Prophetic (Instagram: @daily.prophetic)

"I am so thankful for Natalie as Father God has amplified her voice in this hour of cultural upheaval. This is a great book! I join Natalie in praying for God to anoint men and women to build biblically faithful, God-honoring churches that love people well. When the Church is done right, it's like heaven on earth. There's nothing like it! Thank you, Natalie, for tenderly writing a book that sensitively calls all the prodigals to come back home and enjoy the Father's bountiful love ... in his Church."

Chuck Ramsey, lead pastor of Restoration Church

USA TODAY BESTSELLING AUTHOR

NATALIE RUNION

THE HOUSE THAT JESUS BUILT

LEADING OUR CHURCHES BACK TO GOD'S ORIGINAL BLUEPRINT

DAVID C COOK®

transforming lives together

THE HOUSE THAT JESUS BUILT
Published by David C Cook
4050 Lee Vance Drive
Colorado Springs, CO 80918 U.S.A.

Integrity Music Limited, a Division of David C Cook
Brighton, East Sussex BN1 2RE, England

DAVID C COOK® and related marks are registered trademarks of David C Cook.

The website addresses recommended throughout this book are offered as a
resource to you. These websites are not intended in any way to be or imply an
endorsement on the part of David C Cook, nor do we vouch for their content.

Details in some stories have been changed to protect
the identities of the persons involved.

Bible credits are listed at the end of the book.

Library of Congress Control Number 2024938430
ISBN 978-0-8307-8671-8
eISBN 978-0-8307-8672-5

© 2024 Natalie Ryan Runion
Published in association with the literary agency of Wordserve
Literary Group, Ltd., www.wordserveliterary.com.

The Team: Susan McPherson, Stephanie Bennett, Justin Claypool,
Brian Mellema, James Hershberger, Jack Campbell, Susan Murdock
Cover Design: Joe Cavazos
Cover Author Bio Photo: Ashlee Kay Photography

Printed in the United States of America
First Edition 2024

1 2 3 4 5 6 7 8 9 10

053024

To the Church.
The radical remnant.
The called-out ones.
Let's build something beautiful.

CONTENTS

PART 3—REFRAMING

PREFACE

For the past several years I have led an online community called Raised to Stay: a family of "stayers" from diverse denominations and church experiences around the world. We are leaders, pastors, volunteers, and churchgoers, all wading through the rubble of cultural changes and faith deconstruction, particularly here in our Western church.

Within this online community, I've encountered people from churches who are desperate for healing and hope, those committed to staying even in the wreckage of their disappointment and pain, to be part of rebuilding something that would introduce future generations to churches Jesus himself would want to attend. My first book, *Raised to Stay*, documented my own wondering, wandering, and wrestling with my relationship with the local church as a pastor's kid turned pastor and gave voice to the pain of others in an effort to begin the healing process.

When visiting face to face with pastors and local church leaders, I have come to better understand the challenges many experience who are doing good, godly work in their communities. Being a little further through the journey than some, and always attempting to maintain a prayerful and humble approach, I knew my next book needed to acknowledge some of the areas in our churches where shepherds have compromised the safety of the sheep. And it needed to do this without leaving us in the rubble and by confirming that we do have hope.

The title of this book, *The House That Jesus Built*, encompasses the clear message God gave to me—to bring to his Church—to keep going. I've known God is calling a radical remnant to rise up out of the rubble of deconstruction—not wallow in confusion and defeat—and rebuild with him churches that will serve as cities on a hill in these dark days we live in.

As I spent time in the Scriptures and in prayer, the words on the pages of my Bible jumped out at me—already strategically placed by our God like blueprints for a beautiful cathedral. God's Word from Genesis to Revelation provides us his foundation, floorplan, and framework for a holy, healthy, and safe Church.

And you and I are that Church.

Jesus says in Matthew 16:18–19, "Upon this rock I will build *my church*, and all the powers of hell will not conquer it. And I will give you the keys of the Kingdom of Heaven. Whatever you forbid on earth will be forbidden in heaven, and whatever you permit on earth will be permitted in heaven."

But we are more than a building or a congregation, we are the ekklesia (or ecclesia), the called-out ones, this word coming from *ek*, "out from," and *kaleo*, "to call." In the New Testament the ekklesia is a group of people who are set apart from the world and on mission

to see others come to the saving knowledge of the Gospel of Jesus
Christ. We are that same ekklesia, called out and set apart, not just
once a week when we gather in a physical building, but every single
day as we share the hope of Jesus everywhere we go.

Jesus said he would build the ekklesia, and we, as God's people,
have the opportunity as the called-out to partner with him in
rebuilding something beautiful out of the rubble and back on the
Rock.

As the called-out ones, we must unify and commit to building
on one foundation and one foundation alone: Jesus Christ.

We have the blueprints we need found within the pages of God's
Word. Jesus tells the disciples in Matthew chapter 7:

> Anyone who listens to my teaching and follows it
> is wise, like a person who builds a house on solid
> rock. Though the rain comes in torrents and the
> floodwaters rise and the winds beat against that
> house, it won't collapse because it is built on
> bedrock. But anyone who hears my teaching and
> doesn't obey it is foolish, like a person who builds
> a house on sand. When the rains and floods come
> and the winds beat against that house, it will col-
> lapse with a mighty crash. (vv. 24–27)

We cannot leave Jesus out of our building plans. God's Church
has been nearly destroyed brick by brick by the brutal attacks of our

adversary. Now is the time to rebuild on the only foundation that can withstand and also thrive.

Let's Build Something Beautiful

Though the content in these pages could be applied to any church experience around the world, most of the issues I'll be describing have been observed primarily in the American, or Western, church. I pray wherever you find yourself, your heart will be stirred to see all God's churches healthy, whole, and on mission with the Great Commission and Great Command.

In the first part, we will look at a few challenges that have impacted the overall health of our churches: people-focused platforms and the orphan spirit, along with the effects of spiritual abuse.

Though uncomfortable and convicting, we will stand with our feet in the undeniable ruins of our communities and, through deep personal reflection and prayer, ask ourselves how we as leaders and Christ followers have contributed to at least some of this mess.

As you read this, it's important to understand that while I may at times use language that refers to "the Church" as a whole, *not every* church has felt the effects of deconstruction or experienced spiritual abuse. There are many healthy and thriving churches and leaders who are helping the whole of the Church come together and rebuild itself once again on the sure foundation.

Then in the second and third parts, we will dive into the second chapter of Acts, which describes the birth of the Church and what happened to people who encountered the Holy Spirit in an unexpected way. We will examine our current faulty foundations and misguided frameworks while taking hold of our hammer and sword with great anticipation of reestablishing and protecting churches that Jesus longs to build alongside his people.

God has clearly given us his blueprint. Let's partner with him to rebuild his Church on both biblical formation and Holy Spirit encounter so we can lead a lost world to one name and one name alone: Jesus Christ.

He is coming back soon for a spotless Bride.

He is coming back for his Church. That Church is you and me.

God, may you find us your ready and faithful builders.

INTRODUCTION

"Every house has something wrong with it, Tony! Just pick one, I can't do this anymore," I groaned.

My emotions were getting the better of me, and I knew it. My ever-so-patient husband and I were house hunting in our home state of Kentucky after a six-year hiatus serving at a church in Colorado and I was feeling all the big feelings. I was anxious as we had left our two daughters behind with just four days to find a new home. The pressure was mounting as we went down the list of available real estate on our conservative budget with a ticking clock, crossing off addresses as each home presented a new challenge.

At first, many of our concerns were cosmetic as we dragged our real-estate agent from site to site.

Not enough space. Small backyard. Too close to other homes. Old neighborhood. Wallpaper for days. Dated appliances. No walk-out basement.

Then our attention focused on the bigger nonnegotiable items many don't realize are important until they are about to make an expensive purchase, such as buying a home. These are the potential issues that may go undetected in the initial inspection and then arise a year or so later. They can financially devastate a homeowner.

Cracked foundations. Water in the basement. Termites. Sewage problems. Rotting framework.

As we drove to each available house, it seemed like the ones I loved at first glance ended up being money pits, and I was growing wearier by the day, in fear our family would never have a home like the one we had just sold in Colorado. What if we weren't supposed to move? Had we really heard from God? What if we moved and didn't have anywhere to go?

My father-in-law, with his annoyingly impressive structural engineering experience, would pull in behind us at every home we expressed interest in and begin surveying the property. Kicking concrete, pulling up rocks, looking behind insulation and under porches, and I knew he would find something.

After all, no house is perfect.

I left feeling defeated and frustrated, because even among the imperfections, I could see the good in each one. I envisioned morning coffee on the deck of one house, sleepovers in the bonus room of another, big family holidays in dining rooms and small intimate Bible studies in morning nooks. Yet it felt as if all the bad was outweighing the good the further down the list we went.

Finally, with one day left in our search, our real-estate agent took us to a new build in a brand-new neighborhood. It was by accident really; I had typed in the wrong address of a home we were supposed to see, and it led us to a construction site in a cul-de-sac placed on an acre of Kentucky land. I got out of the car and looked up at the large structure before me, still a shell of what would become our home.

We could see everything: the materials used behind the drywall and under our feet, the dirt that would eventually become a yard, and a cutout of a driveway that would one day hold the cars of our nieces and nephews and friends from school.

I could see it for the house it would become, not the heap of rubble before me.

Unlike the older homes we had seen, I would get to build it with my family, a house that would make new memories and protect us and those we loved, a home that would welcome anyone at any time with a table big enough to seat those looking for a warm meal and good conversation.

My husband and I knew that by deciding to buy the home that day there would be temporary inconveniences. We would have to live on relatives' couches and out of suitcases for six weeks until construction was complete. I would be writing this very book from coffee shops and basements, not a cozy home office as I had the book before. It would have been easy to grow hasty in our search and settle for something that could crumble beneath us because we wanted instant gratification.

I remember standing in the hot summer sun with our builder talking through the final steps of the construction phase. I desperately wanted to move right into our new home upon our family's arrival to Kentucky, but he said something I won't ever forget. "Ma'am, would you like this home built quickly or correctly?"

Suddenly, building a home felt serious. He was right. He could bring in workers to do the job halfway, but a year later we would suffer the consequences of my impatience. There were codes and processes that needed to be met and followed, and it was his job to

ensure every brick was laid with care, not hurried because the own-
ers were bullying him to finish the job before it was time.

I happened to be writing this very book you are holding at the
time, and it struck me that building a new home is a practical illus-
tration of what it looks like to build a church, if not physically, then
spiritually. If you were to go back and reread the very beginning of
this introduction and replace "house" or "home" with "church," it
would make sense.

But it's more than just finding a new physical church building to
attend each week. After all, there are so many options to choose from
when looking for a place of worship we're bound to find some place we
can hide out in the back row. Much like building or buying a home,
we can open our phones and search for churches based on location,
size of congregation, denomination, or music style. We can choose
traditional, contemporary, or art deco exteriors, and even if we want
pews or regular chairs. Want a storefront church in the city? Not only
will you find the church address and website, but you'll also see honest
reviews and critiques galore before you even pull into the parking lot.

I have been around the world visiting churches, and I can assure
you that this conversation is much greater than simply finding a
physical church building. It's much bigger than that.

The last ten years have brought the largest deconstruction movement the Evangelical Church has seen in our lifetime. Movements
and marketing campaigns coaxing people back into pews are no
longer working. The man-made strategies and plans to get believers
and nonbelievers through their doors aren't as effective as they were
in decades past.

We have been tempted to build on the wrong foundations, and now they are compromised.

Our only option is to acknowledge the damage and invite Jesus back into his home to start the rebuilding process.

This is a season of tearing down broken infrastructures and uprooting from barren soil.

We read in Ecclesiastes chapter 3 that there is a season for everything and in verse 3, "a time to tear down and a time to build up." Deconstruction isn't the end of the Church; it is an opportunity and invitation to rebuild on the foundation of the Church Jesus established alongside our fellow brothers and sisters in the faith desperate to see his Kingdom come on earth as it is in heaven.

Built to Last

Our family eventually moved into our new home, and it took several months to unpack all the boxes and arrange each room. I remember sitting in the living room alone—in the quiet of the late night after everyone had gone to bed—marveling at walls that just a few months prior had been patched drywall and exposed beams. In the now finished space I was safe, I was protected, and the family God had given me was tucked peacefully in their beds knowing that come rain or shine, they had a sure covering.

There is a lost world looking for this same refuge, a safe place with a sure covering where they can rest their weary hearts.

It's time for the Kingdom builders to come out of hiding and begin surveying our current condition, with our blueprint in hand: the Word of God.

Are you ready to partner with Jesus in his Church in a rapidly changing world, carrying a never-changing Gospel?

A blueprint for those seeking first the Kingdom of God here on earth will:

- Begin on the foundation of Jesus Christ.
- Hear the voice of God.
- Teach the Word of God.
- Love God.
- Love people.
- Go and make disciples.

We have everything we need in the Word of God to rebuild our churches on a foundation that is unshakable, immovable, and unwavering in our faith. We don't need to use strategies of this world to be a Church that brings a lost world into the saving grace and knowledge of Jesus Christ. We know what to do and how to do it.

I believe there is a remnant in the aftermath who is willing to grab this blueprint, the Word of God, and start sifting through the rubble.

Jesus says in Luke 6:46–49:

> So why do you keep calling me "Lord, Lord!" when you don't do what I say? I will show you what it's like when someone comes to me, listens to my teaching, and then follows it. It is like a person building a house who digs deep and lays the foundation on solid rock. When the floodwaters

rise and break against that house, it stands firm because it is well built. But anyone who hears and doesn't obey is like a person who builds a house right on the ground, without a foundation. When the floods sweep down against that house, it will collapse into a heap of ruins.

As we navigate these chapters together, I pray the power of the Holy Spirit falls on us like the day of Pentecost. I pray we find ourselves in our private Upper Room through an encounter with the Living God and a deep formation of his Word that doesn't just encourage us but challenges and convicts us toward change. I pray that before we beg God to bring change in the global Church, we seek personal repentance for our part in hurting others, partnering with sin, demanding of others what we ourselves weren't willing to give, and in that repentance, we turn toward the Chief Cornerstone as our own rock and source of strength.

Are you ready, Stayers?

We're about to build something beautiful with Jesus.

PART 1

RUBBLIZATION

BUILDING ON BROKENNESS

Rubblization: during a construction project,
unwanted concrete is broken down into small
pieces that are used in the base for new surfaces.

*"Some of you will rebuild the deserted ruins of your cities. Then you
will be known as a rebuilder of walls and a restorer of homes."*

Isaiah 58:12

Chapter 1

TEARING DOWN CASTLES, BUILDING THE KINGDOM

"One thing is certain: the call of Christ is always a promotion.
Were Christ to call a king from his throne to preach the gospel
to some tribe of aborigines, that king would be elevated above
anything he had known before. Any movement toward Christ
is ascent, and any direction away from Him is down."[1]

A. W. Tozer

Have you ever been to the beach and tried to build a really good sandcastle? It's nearly impossible without the right tools, sand texture, and location. If you're too close to the water, it will get washed away with the ebb and flow of the tide, and if you're too far away in dry sand, it is unable to hold a shape. My family and I have spent many afternoons on the beach with brand-new shovels and buckets in tow only to leave all our work behind in a heap for another family to tackle after countless sinking moats and crumbling towers followed by toddler tears.

One year we arrived to discover a large group sculpting the most intricate sandcastle I had ever seen. From sunrise to sunset they worked tirelessly, obviously not first timers as they came with all the necessary tools and a clear plan to build something magnificent. Throughout the day strangers stopped to marvel at their creation until the sun disappeared behind the sea and the moonlight cast an eerie glow upon their majestic castle.

Early the next morning we returned to find the empire collapsed in a clump of wet, gray sand, with only a few fallen towers still visibly trying to keep above the tide. When other families arrived, the kids tried their best to rebuild it, grabbing their own buckets and shovels to re-create the masterpiece, but their efforts were in vain.

Even a mighty castle built by the hands of professional sand sculptors is on borrowed time—at the mercy of the wind and waves that threaten to eat away at the structure grain by grain—until another builder comes along to use what is left as their foundation.

Sand shifts; it isn't consistent. You can't depend on it to build with or upon.

I confess I am guilty of building my faith on shifting sand and not on the firm foundation of the Gospel of Jesus Christ. I have built my faith on my feelings, emotions, if I get what I want, if God does what I want him to do.

I am guilty of building my ministry on shifting sand. I have built to be popular, influential, for followers, for worldly recognition, and it has made me tired, offended, and lazy.

We, as God's Church, are guilty of building on shifting sand. We have built for numbers, buildings, fame, position, and it has cost us precious lives who have yet to set foot back into a sanctuary.

But our God—the very same Creator who made and counted each grain of sand—doesn't change. He stays the same.

James 1:17 reminds us, "Whatever is good and perfect is a gift coming down to us from God our Father, who created all the lights in the heavens. He never changes or casts a shifting shadow."

We often watch what another man or woman is building. Then seeing what has caught the eye of those passing by, even though it clearly isn't stable, even when we wake up one day to see it has fallen, we will still try to build off another's rubble to re-create it rather than investigate what made it fall.

Many foundations the world offers constantly shift beneath us: money, power, status, and identity. But our God is immovable, he is unshakable, and when we build our faith, our ministry, our churches on him, even the biggest waves and most violent storms won't be able to knock them down.

As the people who make up God's churches, what we choose to build with and upon—both individually and corporately—will determine the stability and safety of the House.

Will we choose to build personal castles on fickle sand,

> **When we build our faith, our churches, on God, even the most violent storms won't knock them down.**

or will we choose to partner with Jesus in building the Kingdom on his firm foundation?

The Upside-Down Kingdom

As we rebuild our churches in this upside-down Kingdom, it's going to challenge many of us, as it's contrary to what we've observed and experienced as both congregants and leaders. Our physical titles and positions are fool's gold because the currency of heaven cannot be weighed or traded.

Eternal assignments rarely offer a public platform, so Kingdom promotion will look like worldly demotion to many. It's impossible to measure influence by the sound of applause when our most important work is done in a holy hush. Nobody will be numbering your followers, but your days will be numbered, so pay attention to what you've been given, not what you might be missing.

Yes, this backward Kingdom will mess you up before it sets you up for success in the eyes of the world.

And maybe that's how we know we are where we belong, when we love a trench more than our talent and a field more than fame. This upside-down Kingdom will shake you up and break you down, but it's here God can begin a new work.

As Eugene Peterson writes in his interpretation of Matthew 20:16, "Here it is again, the Great Reversal: many of the first ending up last, and the last first" (MSG).

When we observe the Acts church, we see clear leadership in Luke, Peter, and the other apostles, but it also says they were in one accord. There was unity among them, and that unity starts with leadership stooping down while raising up others who will partner with them on mission. They were building something together and adding to their numbers daily through prayer, dedicating themselves to scriptures and evangelism.

As I reflect on Paul's words in 1 Corinthians 3:9–11, I am convicted as a follower of Jesus:

> For we are both God's workers. And you are God's field. You are God's building.
>
> Because of God's grace to me, I have laid the foundation like an expert builder. Now others are building on it. But whoever is building on this foundation must be very careful. For no one can lay any foundation other than the one we already have—Jesus Christ.

But as a leader, I am challenged as Paul takes it a step further:

> Anyone who builds on that foundation may use a variety of materials—gold, silver, jewels, wood, hay, or straw. But on the judgment day, fire will reveal what kind of work each builder has done. The fire will show if a person's work has any value. If the work survives, that builder will receive a reward. But if the work is burned up, the builder will suffer great loss. The builder will be saved, but like someone barely escaping through a wall of flames. (vv. 12–15)

There is coming a day when all our work and ministry will be laid open and examined by God to see what exactly we laid on his foundation, and we will be accountable for those we misled—it will all be brought into the light. All the gold, silver, jewels, those materials we used that are meant to withstand the strongest of storms will remain, but all the other things that got mixed in along the way—wood (fame), hay (fortune), or straw (the flesh)—will be burned up on judgment day.

Though it is hard to discern one person's foundation from another here on earth, there is coming a day when it will be very clear who built with Jesus and who built for themselves.

Did we build man-made castles or partner with God in building his Kingdom?

The danger of building with flammable materials is the lives it costs us, no matter how beautiful the building may be. Our church staff are some of the first to recognize what the foundation of their church is built upon, and some churches need a fire extinguisher in every office. Between staff meetings, one-on-one meetings, and conversations among staff, it quickly becomes clear if the house is safe or if there is an impending house fire. And unfortunately, sometimes the only thing we can do is resign and let it burn.

I know that sounds harsh, but we are not called to every battle or emergency. Sometimes, the greatest act of service we can give a church is to walk away and let God deal with what remains inside.

Jesus, Our Firm Foundation

"For what we proclaim is not ourselves, but Jesus Christ as Lord, with ourselves as your servants for Jesus' sake. For God, who said,

'Let light shine out of darkness,' has shone in our hearts to give the light of the knowledge of the glory of God in the face of Jesus Christ."

2 Corinthians 4:5–6 ESV

We read in Scripture that the apostles of Jesus Christ were fighting against systems threatening to crush the foundation of the early Church before it even got started, and it's no different today. They, too, were living in the tension of knowing when to take action and when to wait in different situations and circumstances along their ministry journey. Not too long ago I saw a meme circulating social media that said, "If Paul saw the American Church today, we'd be getting a letter," and it was shared hundreds of thousands of times because it was not only funny but true. A lot has changed since Paul's missionary journeys, but as people we haven't changed all that much.

As fallen humans, imperfect Christians, we will all be tempted to steal glory that doesn't belong to us, and God is patient, but not unaware.

Paul writes in 1 Corinthians 3:5–8:

> After all, who is Apollos? Who is Paul? We are only God's servants through whom you believed the Good News. Each of us did the work the Lord gave us. I planted the seed in your hearts, and Apollos watered it, but it was God who made it grow. It's not important who does the planting, or who does the watering. What's important is that God makes the seed grow. The one who plants and the one who waters work together with the same

purpose. And both will be rewarded for their own
hard work.

How quickly we fall for the lie that we are the heroes in our
stories and to the Church. Our churches belong to God, he is the
one who makes them grow and flourish as we, his humble servants,
carry his message of salvation to a lost and dying world. In Matthew
chapter 3, John the Baptist puts it like this: "I baptize with water
those who repent of their sins and turn to God. But someone is coming soon who is greater than I am—so much greater that I'm not
worthy even to be his slave and carry his sandals" (v. 11).

John the Baptist knew it wouldn't be his name, his platform, his
talent, or his ministry that would build the Kingdom. It would be as
a harbinger of Jesus Christ, not in competition with Jesus Christ,
that he would partner with the one true Savior in preparing the
way of his arrival. John understood his assignment and the honor it
was to be a voice declaring in the wilderness, "Prepare ye the way of
the Lord" (Mark 1:3 KJV).

Can you imagine what we could build together if every stone we
laid was intentional in making the path straight for the arrival of
the Holy Spirit? How would our staff meetings,

> **What could we build together if every stone we laid was intentional in making the path straight for the arrival of the Holy Spirit?**

church services, outreach programs, and personal lives change if we saw ourselves as humble harbingers of Jesus Christ?

Though it reads beautifully here on paper, execution of such a concept will require a construction project our earthly church budgets cannot afford. It will cost us our pride, personal agendas, and dreams of the flesh that God has never breathed life upon. It will mean restructuring systems and reevaluating the sacred cows in our denominations and organizations that have served the elite. This biblical concept of being an ambassador of Christ will require showing the original blueprints to many who have been hardened into self-preservation and personal gain, profiting off the movement of Jesus rather than humbly carrying the message of Jesus.

The psalmist writes in Psalm 84:10, "A single day in your courts is better than a thousand anywhere else! I would rather be a gate-keeper in the house of my God than live the good life in the homes of the wicked."

God is scouring the earth looking for the "I would rather" generation who will stand at the gates of our churches and understand their assignment to be a voice in the wilderness declaring the arrival of Jesus Christ to those looking for hope.

Who are the "I would rather" builders of our day who are more interested in keeping watch over the House of God and protecting those inside than owning the House of God and gatekeeping who can enter or participate?

I want to join in the John the Baptist generations who have worked faithfully before us who understood Jesus is the only foundation to build on and stand upon. I want to be like the one Isaiah writes about, as told in Mark chapter 1:1–3, who will be a messenger sent by God, who looks a little wild, a little untamed, a bit unruly but is a voice emerging from the wilderness declaring the arrival of our Jesus.

I want to be a generation of holy harbingers, the prophetic voices in the Church. We may be called divisive, escalating, fear-filled, critical, but we will be the ones carrying the Word of God to edify, exhort, and encourage those looking for hope. These voices will also warn against such things tearing up our foundations and devouring the sheep, and it is vital you and I know the Word of God and the voice of God to discern the true prophetic voices from cheap imitations.

We must know the voice of God to test the many voices screaming into our lives.

Keep using your voice, those emerging from the wilderness, to declare a coming King and a message of hope as well as a warning to get our houses ready for his return. I know it feels lonely, but you aren't alone and God is raising up a generation of forerunners and separating those bearing his fruit from those growing their own.

> I baptize with water those who repent of their sins and turn to God. But someone is coming soon who is greater than I am—so much greater that I'm not worthy even to be his slave and carry his sandals. He will baptize you with the Holy Spirit and with fire. He is ready to separate the chaff from the wheat with his winnowing fork. Then he will clean up the threshing area, gathering the wheat into his barn but burning the chaff with never-ending fire. (Matt. 3:11–12)

Fireproof

I want to be fireproof. I want to have full confidence that the message I am carrying, the roles I step into, the leaders I partner with, and the churches I attend are part of the wheat God is gathering into his barn.

Let all the other stuff burn. Anything that isn't producing fruit, any opportunity that doesn't align with his Kingdom, any dream or desire of mine that isn't from God, I pray will be pruned from my fickle heart and separated with his winnowing fork so I will bear a good harvest in every season.

I've observed my peers forced to leave church staff or ministry organizations because they found themselves in a burning field of another person's chaff, not realizing they had partnered with or been under the leadership of someone building a personal empire. They were Kingdom people who thought they were doing Kingdom work only to find they were hired to be a servant of a self-appointed king.

They have felt managed and disposable, not mentored or discipled. When leaders build for their own benefit, everyone who is hired and fired becomes a commodity. Our churches begin to operate as an organization and leaders as CEOs and the target for success is constantly moving depending on who is holding the hammer. Suddenly, we're no longer hiring pastors and those called to shepherd the people of God, we're hiring those who will make leadership look good. It's easy to spot and hire talent to give the people what they want. In the business world recruiters do this every day for the benefit of a company or organization. They headhunt, recruit, hire, and release their new hirelings into the wild with a job description and a "May the odds be forever in your favor."

But our churches aren't the world.

I have been hired by pastors for positions that ultimately uprooted my family from our home and everything we knew, and we were scared. They would rave about my experience, love for the church, and powerful leadership on and off the platform that was unique and prophetic. I loved that they saw my heart to shepherd both with and without a microphone. Being a worship pastor always requires a level of talent and skill to execute the job, but I knew much of what I would be doing would involve pastoring staff and congregants.

With each church and role, both my husband and I knew when my season was coming to an end, as leadership became critical of the very attributes that had brought me into the position.

I call this the "wheel of favor," as people are set up high on the wheel upon their arrival, used for every event and service until someone the leaders like better shows up. Seats shift, the wheel revolves until you don't recognize anyone anymore in leadership's attempt to find the perfect combination or team that doesn't exist. All you're left with are staff and volunteers vying for the top seat and willing to do whatever they need to do to remain in that position, while wounded riders have no idea why they got bumped off.

I hadn't changed; the tone of my voice, the way I led the congregation, the posture upon which I led the team and heart for ministry were the same as the day they hired me. However, when the target of talent and personal preference is constantly moving, people become collateral damage in the process. Somewhere along the way, they changed their minds about me. Suddenly, I was too much, too loud, too big, and the more I was critiqued, the more mistakes I made until I was a shell of the person I was when I arrived.

They didn't just break my heart; my spirit was crushed.

Maybe your heart and spirit have been broken too.

For the brokenhearted, I have good news for us: God doesn't change his mind about us. I'm so thankful his target doesn't move and we can wake up every day knowing though we might miss the mark, he offers us love and mercy and grace upon grace!

As pastors and ministry leaders, when we hire people, we expect them to do the jobs they are hired to do, but we also have a responsibility to shepherd those we bring on staff. We want their talent, but many pastors aren't trained in organizational leadership and find themselves holding a real life, a real family, and a holy calling in their hands.

We are holding a human, a child of God, an anointed man or woman who isn't a hireling but someone with a mantle that must be stewarded and served. God won't continue entrusting us with anointed leaders if we don't love and nurture those he has already given us.

This doesn't mean we have to personally hold their hands or even personally oversee them; it means we have healthy leaders in place who can help us develop a staff culture of honor, purpose, and mission focused on the person, not just their position.

Before hiring someone for their talent, before asking them to leave a current position, to uproot their families, ask yourself if you are the best leader for them, if the church is in a good place to steward their anointing, and if you can help birth what God is growing inside of them even if it doesn't directly benefit you or the ministry.

We can't just pastor from our platforms. We should be personally pastoring a nervous new youth pastor in our office who just received a scary email from an enraged parent. We should be caring for the worship leader who messed up in front of the entire congregation and is mortified and now questioning their calling. We should be shepherding the new staff member who didn't realize church staff still gossip and talk behind your back and who feels betrayed by this revelation.

If we hire them, we must pastor them. Yes, they may have gone to seminary or Bible college, but knowledge doesn't equal discipleship. Many times, those we are leading aren't looking for instruction alone, they are looking for friendship and mentorship.

Paul wrote to the church of Corinth in 1 Corinthians 4:14–16, "I am not writing these things to shame you, but to warn you as my beloved children. For even if you had ten thousand others to teach you about Christ, you have only one spiritual father. For I became your father in Christ Jesus when I preached the Good News to you. So I urge you to imitate me."

> **May our prayer be that in all things we see Jesus in every detail.**

As we take a tour of the Church together in these pages, from the foundation to the framework to the floorplan, may our prayer be that in all things we see Jesus in every detail. He is our master builder, our cornerstone, our Great Architect. May we imitate him in everything we do as we introduce others to a Church he has built where they will find refuge and hope.

Reflection Prayer

"Heavenly Father, please forgive me for building my life on anything but you. Forgive me for building fast because I wanted to get ahead, forgive me for desiring popularity or influence when you have given me authority to carry your Gospel in your Name. Jesus, I want to build my life on you, my Firm Foundation. Every gift, every talent, every good thing I have has come from you and it is an honor to partner with you in this Kingdom work. Amen."

Chapter 2

A HOLY HOUSE CLEANING

"But among you it will be different. Whoever wants to be a leader among you must be your servant, and whoever wants to be first among you must become your slave. For even the Son of Man came not to be served but to serve others and to give his life as a ransom for many."

Matthew 20:26–28

I stood in the middle of my best friend's living room watching her clean like a crazy person. We had been planning this lunch for months, and from the looks of my friend covered in spit-up and wearing flannel PJ pants, this felt more like an intervention than a girls' day out. She was throwing stuffed animals into bins, bottles into the sink, wiping up her coffee table with a dirty burp cloth, and asking me to hand her the one rogue shoe lying at my feet.

As I tossed her the toddler-sized Converse, I asked, "Why are you cleaning up before the cleaners come?" She jerked her head up, using her lower lip to blow wispy bangs out of her eyes that were now dramatically rolling out of her head as she replied, "Natalie, I have to clean before they get here so they don't see how I really live."

Oh Church, we aren't so different from my spit-up-covered bestie in her two-day-old pj's. We want desperately to present a perfect House to our Sunday-morning family, going to great lengths to do a quick cleanup on Saturday night, when the truth is, there are parts rotting from the inside out and we hope nobody will catch the stench. We're throwing the sins of leaders under our rugs and in some cases aiding and abetting abusers hoping nobody will notice, but somebody always gets tripped up because God doesn't want a clean house, he demands a Holy House.

If we're going to rebuild from the ruins, we're going to need to do some deep house cleaning and throw out what has been rotting our foundation and compromising the safety of the sheep. But God is the Housekeeper, he holds all the keys. So let's roll up our sleeves because we've got a day of pitching some things into the dumpster ahead of us.

The OG Stayers

The book of Acts has always been one of my favorite books of the Bible. I love watching the very first Church be built before our very eyes, those who knew Jesus and those who would join their mission of taking the Gospel of Jesus far and wide.

Though the Bible offers us a book-by-book blueprint for Kingdom establishing and Church building, the book of Acts gives us a crash course directly from the mouth of one who witnessed the birth of the first Church. Luke, the author of Acts, sets the stage for us in our time together:

So they left the mountain called Olives and returned to Jerusalem. It was a little over half a mile. They went to the upper room they had been using as a meeting place: Peter, John, James, Andrew, Philip, Thomas, Bartholomew, Matthew, James, son of Alphaeus, Simon the Zealot, Judas, son of James. They *agreed they were in this for good*, completely together in prayer, the women included. Also Jesus' mother, Mary, and his brothers. (Acts 1:12–14 MSG)

They agreed they were in this for good.

Reader, meet the original stayers.

The very first Church was committed to staying in position and to the mission of Jesus Christ, unified on a foundation of corporate prayer, among other key foundational components. I have never attended a corporate prayer meeting and wished I had spent my time doing something else. Prayer cleans out the clutter in our own hearts, it makes room for more of the Holy Spirit and repositions us from navel gazing to fixing our eyes back on Jesus.

I remember one year, a church I served on staff dedicated every Wednesday to host prayer meetings at different points of the day. It felt so tedious putting together all the teams and worship sets, and if I'm honest, I would often feel a sense of dread in the disruption of my daily staff responsibilities. However, the moment we were all in that room shoulder to shoulder, worshipping and praying, that inconvenience turned to intercession and there was no other place I wanted to be.

We were in this together for good.

There were those who came in off the street, seeing a full parking lot and the prayer-room light shining from the road. They'd sneak in the back door, remove their hats, slip their purses onto the floor, and find a place to kneel. Microphones sat at the front of the room for anyone to come up and pray, and one by one, with meekness and tenderness, men and women as well as teens and young children would share a scripture or prayer.

> **Prayer reminds us of our foundation when it feels as if the world beneath us might crumble.**

One evening, a man whom I had never seen before with a long white beard and bushy eyebrows took the mic and stood quiet for several moments before a sob escaped his throat. The room grew silent as he shared his wife had just passed away. He confessed loneliness and deep grief and the impact the prayer meetings and those who had gathered were having on his life. The people of God gathered around him as he stood, shoulders hunched, his face in his hands, weeping. There wasn't a dry eye in the room.

Prayer reminds us of our foundation when it feels as if the world beneath us might crumble, when grief might overtake us, when loss may leave us hopeless. It takes us back to the feet of Jesus where we're reminded of a God who, from Creation, has wanted to hear from his children.

A House of Prayer

In this first chapter of Acts we see the disciples who had spent around three years with Jesus and been taught the power of prayer through his teaching and example. They knew the only way to have a healthy and holy church was to be a house built on prayer.

Back in Matthew 21, Jesus arrived at the temple and drove out all the people who were buying and selling, as he flipped tables and said, "'My Temple will be called a house of prayer,' but you have turned it into a den of thieves!" (v. 13).

There is an appropriate time to clear out anything in our churches that is contradictory to the Word of God and God's intention for his House, but so many times we make excuses for the mess rather than doing a holy house cleaning.

Much like a family might do for a loved one in an episode of one of those hoarder documentaries, it does us good as the people of God to take inventory of what is cluttering the spiritual rooms of our churches, and our own temples, as well as the idols we've gathered over time.

I am convicted that I have laid false worship on the altar only to find it to be worthless worship.

Our churches have also picked up a few things cluttering our altars:

- fame
- money
- consumerism
- prosperity gospel

- harmful theology
- politics
- discrimination
- sexism

In Malachi, God was clear he wanted only pure, worthy sacrifices:

> "How I wish one of you would shut the Temple doors so that these worthless sacrifices could not be offered! I am not pleased with you," says the LORD of Heaven's Armies, "and I will not accept your offerings. But my name is honored by people of other nations from morning till night. All around the world they offer sweet incense and pure offerings in honor of my name. For my name is great among the nations," says the LORD of Heaven's Armies. (1:10–11)

And if that doesn't make one squirm in their seat, God finished his rebuke with this bone-chilling mic drop:

> "Cursed is the cheat who promises to give a fine ram from his flock but then sacrifices a defective one to the Lord. For I am a great king," says the LORD of Heaven's Armies, "and my name is feared among the nations!" (v. 14)

God was so weary with their defective worship that he begged someone to shut the doors.

This Old Testament passage is God's rebuke of the Israelites who provided flawed or undignified animals as worship and his rebuke to the priest for accepting them. The Israelites had pleaded with God to intervene, and when he did, some showed up with a blemished animal, these "cheats" too lazy to find a proper sacrifice.

I am sure you could add other items to this list of junk our churches have collected from the world that hold no place in the House of God. Prayer helps in guiding us in the process of discerning what should stay and what needs to go, it reveals our lazy sacrifices and compels us to bring only what is pure and of God.

It helps us know what needs to be deconstructed so we can reconstruct on solid ground.

As we begin the daunting task of clearing out the cobwebs in the back corners of our churches, my prayer is we will begin to uncover vital foundational building blocks we can use for God's glory.

Radical Generosity

I can usually discern that I am in a healthy church because it is a praying church, but along with being a praying church, it is a generous church. I don't mean only in their finances, I am talking about being generous with their resources, time, accessibility, and care for those they serve.

As we continue in these pages together, we will see many elements that brought about the establishment of the church of Acts, one of those being radical generosity. Acts chapter 2:44–46 tells us, "And all the believers met together in one place and shared everything they had. They sold their property and possessions and shared the money with those in need. They worshiped together at the Temple each day, met in homes for the Lord's Supper, and shared their meals with great joy and generosity."

"They shared everything they had."

What might this look like for us in the modern-day church? It's quite simple, actually.

As I visit churches in every type of demographic and landscape, I see their radical generosity in those sharing their homes, meals, and lives with me while I'm in their care. I am given a warm bed, a hot meal, a roof over my head, and sweet conversation by fireplaces with the family of God. When I enter these homes, I am instantly shown a picture of a generous God through his generous people that I will one day sing beside around the throne in eternity. Sharing what they have, giving what they can, and inviting me into their homes much like John Mark's mom, Mary, did in the early Church by opening her home for them to gather.

Part of being radically generous as the Church is being responsible with the tithes, offerings, and gifts being brought into the storehouse each week. God is watching how we steward what others are bringing in as an act of worship.

I'll never forget the first email I received from our accounting department while working for a large church. I was planning a big event for my department and wanted to pull out all the stops to ensure it was successful and one to remember. When I submitted my budget, our head accountant questioned some of the items on my list and in a gentle rebuke simply reminded me, "We are spending people's worship." That was his signature line on all his emails to the church staff, reminding us that what we were spending was costly and holy.

It is very important to know that the church we choose to call home, the church we choose to serve on staff, isn't hiding anything financially. If every staff party is a carnival with extravagant gifts and fanfare, if money is being spent without any accountability, if there isn't an elder or organization holding the pastor and church to a budget who has access to bank statements and every penny being spent, that is a red flag.

> When we build on Jesus, the sheep will know the sound of their shepherd's voice and return to a field they trust.

Congregants, we have a responsibility to be Kingdom bringers, not earthly consumers.

Pastors, we might have the charisma and money to build something fancy, but we have an even greater responsibility to build with godly wisdom.

When we build on Jesus, the sheep will know the sound of their shepherd's voice and return to a field they trust.

Are our churches safe places for sheep looking for refuge?

If You Build It, They Will Come

Don't get me wrong, I like hot coffee and padded chairs as much as anyone, and after growing up in churches with under three hundred people, I appreciate things like air-conditioning, clean accommodations, and paved parking lots. However, I'm afraid we've become quite comfortable and we're losing reverence for the House of God when we speak of her leaders and people as if they work for us. We've become consumers with quick fingers to rate sermons like we're rating an Airbnb behind anonymous screen names.

In a world where we can get anything we want on demand delivered to our doorstep without ever taking out our contact lenses or changing out of our pajamas, it's no wonder we have a culture who wants the same from our churches.

> **If we aren't walking into every gathering of believers like we're walking onto a training field next to fellow soldiers fighting against the same enemy, we've already lost the battle.**

Give it to me now.

This is what I want and when I want it.

This is how I want it done.

I'm a tithe-paying customer.

You work for me.

Though not every Christian is demanding a platform or position in their church, many have strong opinions about the way the church is run, and they use their money and status to try to bully leadership into doing things their way.

Before social media and Google reviews, congregants would leave anonymous notes in offering plates making their demands known. From whom they wanted to preach to opinions on carpet color and music selection, people have turned the sanctuary of our God into a clubhouse taking reservations and I believe it grieves the heart of our Father.

Consumer Christianity isn't new; since the fall in the garden humans have been selfish, demanding, and inward focused. Like a baby who depends on its mother for every nutrient, we also want to be soothed, coddled, and swaddled. Though we are all spiritual infants for a time, the hope is that we will grow up and become less dependent on our churches to feed us milk and we will crave something more from the Lord and his Word.

The author of Hebrews writes:

> There is much more we would like to say about this, but it is difficult to explain, especially since you are spiritually dull and don't seem to listen. You have been believers so long now that you ought to be teaching others. Instead, you need someone to teach you again the basic things about God's word. You are like babies who need milk and cannot eat solid food. For someone who lives on milk is still an infant and doesn't know how to do what is right. Solid food is for those who are mature, who through training have the skill to recognize the difference between right and wrong. (5:11–14)

To rebuild, we must change our posture and attitude toward the role of our churches in our personal lives. If we aren't walking into every gathering of believers like we're walking onto a training field next to fellow soldiers fighting against the same enemy, we've already lost the battle.

Let's take a moment together to go back to the basics of God's original intent for the Church:

The Church is a dwelling place for the Spirit of God (Eph. 2:20–22).

The Church does not exist for us, it exists as a dwelling place for the Spirit of God and to encourage and edify the saints as a common place of worship. God does not serve us, we serve him, and we do everything we do as if unto the Lord, not for our own benefit or gain.

God's temple is holy, and we are that temple (1 Cor. 3:17).

We, the people of God, are the Church. When we say the Church hurt us, that isn't a wrong statement because the Church is made up of people who hurt us. It doesn't matter if we are physically standing in a cathedral or building with "church" on the sign, wherever we go, we are God's Church. We represent him, we represent the family of God. We are to love people wherever we go, because wherever we go, we are in active ministry on mission with the Great Commission. We are the temple of the Almighty God, even on social media and in traffic and waiting to get our oil changed at the local mechanic. Let us not forget that we are to be set apart because the Living God dwells in us.

We have an active role and position in the family of God, and Jesus Christ is our firm foundation. When we build everything we do on that foundation and build together for the glory of the Lord, there is blessing in the unity of the gathered saints.

We are called to equip, not complain, or compare or compete (Eph. 4:12).

Did you know that the average church staff spends nearly three hours of their eight-hour day talking about ministry in problem mode rather than problem-solving mode? I was recently listening to Cy Wakeman, founder and CEO of Reality-Based Leadership, on a leadership podcast and she said, "We talk more about our people than we do to them."

Imagine if we stepped into our calling to equip and also protect one another by challenging unhealthy and abusive systems. What would it look like to take those hours we spend complaining over coffee about that staff person or leader and become to others the leader that we need? What if instead of tearing one another down, we chose to build something beautiful together?

There is a world looking to us for a Living Hope in a life of despair and we cannot afford to grow weary in doing good.

We read in Hebrews 6:10, "For God is not unjust. He will not forget how hard you have worked for him and how you have shown your love to him by caring for other believers."

God sees you, remain on mission.

A Church on Mission and Commission

What is that mission? It's the Great Commission and it comes with a strategic blueprint to build with Jesus.

If you're wondering where to start, Jesus has given us the first few building blocks right here in this passage:

> Jesus, undeterred, went right ahead and gave his charge: "God authorized and commanded me to commission you: Go out and train everyone you meet, far and near, in this way of life, marking them by baptism in the threefold name: Father, Son, and Holy Spirit. Then instruct them in the practice of all I have commanded you. I'll be with you as you do this, day after day after day, right up to the end of the age." (Matt. 28:18–20 MSG)

GO

TRAIN and EQUIP

BAPTIZE

TEACH

One year in college I went on a ministry trip with Campus Crusade for Christ. We went door to door sharing the message of Jesus Christ, handing out Bibles and bags of food. As a pastor's kid you might think I was a natural, but in fact, I was the most inexperienced and timid on our team. My peers, many of whom had come to know Jesus in high school or even more recently, were on fire. They were comfortable walking up to perfect strangers and telling them about a God who loved them.

I was embarrassed at how little I actually knew about my faith. It challenged me to study the Word of God more and become better at articulating the Gospel of Jesus without relying only on talking about church or being a pastor's kid. In the process of telling other people about my Jesus, I fell back in love with him.

When is the last time you have personally shared the message of Jesus Christ with someone? When is the last time you've prayed with someone to make Jesus Christ Lord and Savior of their life? This isn't a guilt trip or to make anyone feel like a bad Christian. When we spend so much of our lives in one church or in one ministry, it's easy to grow complacent in just playing church and looking the part we are supposed to play.

How do we stay and not grow stale?

You will fall back in love with Jesus by taking the risk to tell others about him, and you will fall back in love with the Church when you take the risk to invite others in who are looking for a place to call home.

Let's Keep It Clean

Now that I'm a mom, I understand my own mother wasn't crazy, she was tired. I now know why she wanted the house to be clean when she came home from a twelve-hour shift at work: she didn't want to spend her evening cleaning up after my sister and me. It must have been frustrating for her to spend at least half of her day off on her hands and knees scrubbing floors only to have us run through, dropping backpacks and shoes in our wake, on our way to the couch to watch after-school specials and destroy her nicely fluffed pillows.

The hardest part of keeping a house clean is not letting the clutter build up again. Once we empty the junk drawer, it needs to be repurposed for something other than throwing in items we're too lazy to find proper places for, such as the random rubber band, chip clip, or failed homework assignment.

It's easy to sit in a staff meeting and talk about all the things that need to be cleaned, make the lists, and do a quick wipe-down to make it appear as if the junk has been hauled away. But so often we just replace it with more junk, because let's be honest, we can be lazy people.

For a true purge in our churches to be effective, the changes should start with those of us who are on the inside of the House each and every day. We should be willing to call sin out, expose the dark hallways, and shed light on the areas that have been covered by those not willing to get their hands dirty.

How do we start this holy house cleaning?

We learn from the first part of Acts and we first commit to not quitting. No matter how messy, no matter how dirty it may be, we're in this together and we aren't going to keep covering up all the religious junk that looked as if it had purpose but was cluttering the House. Does this mean staying in a toxic church or under abusive leadership? Absolutely not! As I mentioned earlier, sometimes the healthiest thing we can do to stay with Jesus is leave a church and let God handle what remains.

This is why we must devote ourselves to prayer and intercession, asking God to give us discernment and grace for the days ahead.

Not everyone will admit their house is dirty.

But I pray God gives his white glove to some saints willing to do some deep cleaning who aren't afraid to walk through a door that has been closed on them and reveal the evidence everyone else wants to ignore.

We start with our own temple, our own heart, and then move to the House of God. One day at a time, one heart at a time, one church at a time.

Reflection Prayer

"Heavenly Father, I pray to be a temple of your Holy Spirit, that you would do a holy house cleaning in my life. Show me where I have hidden sin, temptation, unforgiveness, and anything else that might be cluttering my life. Forgive me for trying to look like I have everything together and not allowing you into certain areas I know are unkept. I give you full control of every room in my house; cleanse me and give me clean hands and a pure heart. Amen."

Chapter 3

IT'S A HARD KNOCK LIFE

"This resurrection life you received from God is not a timid, grave-tending life. It's adventurously expectant, greeting God with a childlike 'What's next, Papa?' God's Spirit touches our spirits and confirms who we really are. We know who he is, and we know who we are: Father and children. And we know we are going to get what's coming to us—an unbelievable inheritance!"

Romans 8:15–17 MSG

The hot Haitian sun beat down on our metal tap-tap as we bounced along the dirt road of a small town just outside Port-au-Prince, Haiti. My hands wrapped around the metal bars and I squinted into the high noon sun as we came to a slow stop, our driver pointing toward a large piece of land stretching on for miles.

Through a translator we learned we were at a mass burial site of those who had lost their lives in the January 2010 earthquake that hit just outside of the Haitian capital of Port-au-Prince, measuring a magnitude of 7.0, killing an estimated 300,000 people, displacing millions. A hush fell over our mission's team as we silently surveyed the rolling hills that held precious remains.

Children were gathered in their Sunday best at the entrance, some playing together and others sitting somberly in the soft earth as they traced their fingers into the dirt.

"Are these children here to visit those they lost in the earthquake?" I asked the translator as he helped us out of the back of the truck.

"No," he responded in a solemn tone. "These children come every Sunday to wait for their parents to return."

I stood speechless at this gate that separated childlike faith from the cruel reality of death. To this day his words still echo in my heart and mind, the image of those children in their suits and dresses standing in the scorching heat holding on to hope seared into my soul. They had not only witnessed but also survived one of the greatest natural disasters ever to be recorded in history. Despite the loss and trauma, they climbed through the rubble of their city each week to stand at the edge of destruction, believing those who had been lost would be found and come back for them.

Over the last fifteen years our churches have experienced a seismic shift that has shaken the Body of Christ to her very core, and we are now left to sift through the rubble of church hurt, anger, offense, frustration, and fear. Barna reports, "More than 4,000 churches closed in America in 2020. Over that same time, over 20,000 pastors left the ministry and 50 percent of current pastors say they would leave the ministry if they had another way of making a living."[2]

The statistics also include congregants and those who call them-selves Christ followers, stating, "Monthly, committed churchgoers are now about half as common as they were two decades ago ... *the share of practicing Christians has nearly dropped in half since 2000.*"[3]

As discouraging as these numbers may be, we must not grow weary in doing good. God has given us his Church, as imperfect as she may be, as a safehouse where we will meet spiritual orphans looking for life among the ruins. It is our honor and responsibility to meet them where they are and offer them Jesus, the Living Hope.

The apostle Paul writes in Ephesians 2:19–22:

> So now you Gentiles are no longer strangers and foreigners. You are citizens along with all of God's holy people. You are members of God's family. Together, we are his house, built on the founda-tion of the apostles and the prophets. And the cornerstone is Christ Jesus himself. We are care-fully joined together in him, becoming a holy temple for the Lord. Through him you Gentiles are also being made part of this dwelling where God lives by his Spirit.

As we dive into this next section of the book, I want to be very clear that this term *spiritual orphan* is in no way used in tandem or in association with one who has been orphaned by biological par-ents. It isn't meant to diminish the experiences and testimonies of those who have gone through the foster system or adoption process.

There is a very real distinction between one who has been physically orphaned and one struggling with the orphan spirit.

The orphan spirit causes one to dwell in a constant state of abandonment, rejection, and disappointment. It attacks the mind with feelings of fear, worry, and anxiety, causing someone to see everything through a lens of lack, creating a poverty mindset that there is never enough for them. It's only through the truth of the Word of God that this spirit can be replaced with the Spirit of God that speaks of who we are in Christ: loved, adopted, accepted, and lacking nothing.

Just as those sweet Haitian orphans sat at the fence with great anticipation for someone to take them home, we as God's Church—the people and our local church buildings—have an opportunity to welcome the foreigner, stranger, and fatherless into our homes where they can find shelter and an imperfect family loved by a perfect Heavenly Father.

> The orphan spirit causes one to dwell in a constant state of abandonment, rejection, and disappointment.

However, to be that safe place for the lost and weary, we must be willing to acknowledge where our foundation has been compromised, the parts of our framework that have been weakened, and repent for building our churches on anything and everything apart from our Chief Cornerstone, Jesus Christ.

If we were to look over our own personal journey with the big-C Church, many of us could pinpoint where we saw the cracks begin to form. They seemed small at first as we wrestled to master new technological advances, cultural shifts, and social media. Pastors and leaders went from tending to their sheep in the House of God to being politicians, celebrities, and social media influencers.

And the sheep lost shepherds.

Spiritual orphans lost mothers and fathers.

Those tiny cracks in our foundation suddenly became structural emergencies, yet we weren't willing to admit that what we had built wasn't able to hold what we were cramming into our buildings.

We have tried to look like the world.

We have used the same materials, strategies, blueprints, and marketing campaigns, yet we forget that what we win people with is what we will have to continue offering to keep them, and the human heart is fickle.

Jesus didn't need antics or campaigns to build anything to bring people to his message of salvation.

The Word of God was enough for Jesus.

The Word of God is enough for us as his Church today.

Just as the Lord assured Jeremiah that if he was obedient to speak God's Word he wouldn't have to be afraid of anyone or anything, we can have that same confidence. When we walk in obedience to do and say exactly what God has given us to say and do, God will "appoint us over nations and kingdoms to uproot and tear down, to destroy and overthrow, to build and to plant" (Jer. 1:10 NIV).

Everything he asks us to uproot will prepare the ground for a new harvest.

The enemy would like nothing more than for the people of God to walk away, quit, and leave our positions, but God isn't finished with his Church or with us. He has hard and holy work for us to do as he hands us the blueprints to rebuild on a new foundation, an architectural plan that can be found in his Word. Jesus, the stone that the builders rejected, our Chief Cornerstone, is where we start, keeping our eyes fixed on him to ensure every line is straight and the structure is secure.

The Scriptures are filled with faithful men and women who were willing to build in the physical and spiritual alongside God for Kingdom advancement. These architects in the faith weren't superhuman or special, but they were obedient to go against kings and political systems to build what was asked of them. Sometimes they had clear instruction; other times, God was quiet, but it didn't stop them.

Noah built an ark before a single drop of rain had fallen (Gen. 6:14–22).

Solomon built the first Temple in Jerusalem (1 Kings 6).

Nehemiah rebuilt the city walls of Jerusalem (Neh. 2:11–20).

Rachel and Leah together built the house of Israel (Ruth 4:11).

Every time God asked someone to build something, it cost them something, and in some cases, it cost them their lives.

Jesus teaches the cost of being a disciple in the book of Luke, saying, "But don't begin until you count the cost. For who would begin construction of a building without first calculating the cost to see if there is enough money to finish it?" (14:28).

What God has called us to build here on earth in his Name is too costly to construct on the wrong foundation or to not finish what we start.

Paul writes in 1 Corinthians 3:10–11, "Because of God's grace to me, I have laid the foundation like an expert builder. Now others are building on it. But whoever is building on this foundation must be very careful. For no one can lay any foundation other than the one we already have—Jesus Christ."

Orphan Spirits and Wannabes

In a season of deep rejection in the local church, I became aware of my own orphan spirit. I had come into a new position where the staff had years of relational equity, work rhythms, and processes and I felt as if I were a tiny cog in a giant wheel. Every time I offered a suggestion, tried something new, inserted myself into a conversation, or even tried to lead as I was hired to do, I was met with resistance and indifference. It was in this season I realized how badly I wanted the approval of my peers, even those who were unkind and threatened by me being there. I hated how desperate I was to have a seat at their table and the way their rejection caused me to question my calling.

> In many churches, we have spiritual orphans leading spiritual orphans and we compromise our integrity and convictions to fit in, hurting and excluding others in the process.

I realized that in many churches, we have spiritual orphans leading spiritual orphans and we compromise our integrity and convictions to fit in, hurting and excluding others in the process.

Our churches will often defend the bad behavior of talented leaders who are wrestling with this spirit because they fear losing them, but our churches cannot afford to lose healthy leaders either.

Church leaders and staff are simply sheep with a title or position of leadership who have been educated or trained to serve in a particular office of ministry. It doesn't matter how many degrees we have in theology or leadership, how many churches we've planted or served, how many books we have written, or albums released: we are grossly human.

We are not immune to bad behavior, sin, or hurting those we love and lead. Paul confesses in Romans 7:15, "I don't really understand myself, for I want to do what is right, but I don't do it. Instead, I do what I hate."

I cannot tell you how many Christians message me daily with stories of deep betrayal by a church leader they assumed knew better or whom they believed should at least do better. Imperfect people leading imperfect people is a recipe for disaster, and yet we do it all the time in the corporate world with fewer problems than we see in our churches.

How often we forget that our enemy isn't out to kill, steal, and destroy the world.

He wants to divide and divorce the family of God.

He wants our ministries to die.

He wants to kill us, body, mind, soul.

He wants us to question our identity and calling.

To gossip and slander to feel superior and worthy.

To shoot the wounded and eliminate any competition that might be in our way of getting to where we believe we belong.

This isn't new to current culture or society; the enemy has nothing new under the sun, yet we fall for his antics every time. Plus, with advances in technology and social media, our insecurities are now exacerbated as we take a front-row seat to the lives of our peers. We can see into their homes, families, jobs, churches, and ministries and we wonder why God has given them so much and us so little. Suddenly, our house isn't big enough, our spouse not as attractive, our kids not as gifted and we see the buffet God has set before us as leftover Kingdom scraps.

We complain there isn't enough blessing to go around the table of the Lord.

We look at the plates of our brothers and sisters and wonder why they have more.

When the orphan spirit partners with castle-building Christians, we build an orphanage filled with those desperate for a name rather than churches safe for the true Fatherless.

While speaking at a women's conference, I was given the opportunity to sit on a panel with three other women, one who had grown up without a father. She was a powerhouse worship leader in her thirties, anointed and humble, and I was blown away to learn she had not grown up in church, but was raised by a single mom and found Jesus in her twenties. As a staff member of this church, she sat on the panel to help facilitate questions, and during a small lull in our conversation she gently leaned forward and asked me, "Natalie, you grew up with a supportive father, a pastor. I didn't grow up with a dad. How is it that someone who has such a good example of a dad would still struggle with the orphan spirit?"

The room grew silent at the weight of the moment. One daughter, who had grown up fatherless, another daughter who had grown up with a father and yet both orphaned in different ways. It was a loaded question with a three-minute time limit and all I could say was "Because we're all desperate to be known and even with a good earthly dad and a good Heavenly Father, the enemy still tries to make us feel homeless and unloved."

I'm often asked how we know if we're struggling with this form of oppression that attacks us many times out of the blue. It has been my experience that most Christians struggle with the orphan spirit at one time or another. It's certainly alive and well in our churches and partially responsible for some of the abuse we see from church leaders. A need for power, control, and validity leading those looking for a father figure in a fatherless society.

In a recent Instagram post regarding the orphan spirit, Nate Johnston warned those under the sound of his voice to "be weary who you are connecting and running with," encouraging them to "find people with little fanfare that love Jesus."

He then gave examples of what to look for in those operating in this spirit, such as "territorial, they always have to 'one up' you in revelation and insight, they name drop, they love gossip, give frequent warning words to those they are threatened by, steal/highjack other's movements and creativity, and they need to be the main attraction in any greenroom or superhero in any scenario," to name a few characteristics in his very lengthy list.

I don't know about you, but I can see myself in more than one of those on that list throughout my life, and even now my prayer is "Search me, oh God. If there is any wickedness in me, any remains of this spirit in my life, forgive me and cleanse me by your power and grace. I want to walk in the fullness of who I am in you and you alone."

More Upper Rooms, Fewer Greenrooms

I'll never forget one particular post I shared in the Raised to Stay online community that blew up overnight. I simply wrote, "If we're going to deconstruct our churches, let's start with greenrooms."

What began as an innocent conversation starter opened an evangelical first-world Pandora's box that left many believers and church leaders scratching their heads. Out of all the challenging conversations I had started in the years Raised to Stay had been active, from church abuse to losing our friends to church hurt, we had never received this kind of divisive and emotional response.

It isn't uncommon for a church to have a room off the platform with water and things a pastor or other leaders might need before heading out to lead the people of God. I have seen greenrooms used well by churches around the world in my travels and see their value at conferences where a church is hosting a special guest and their families, often including small children, providing a safe and hospitable environment.

Regardless of the name of the room or how a church might use it, it was the response of the Christian community to this particular post that grieved my heart. The spiritual orphans came running to the gate to defend their position, many from a place of fear that if this one space that gave them identity and purpose were compromised, they would become nameless and faceless once again.

There was a yucky pride in those who longed to feel special and exclusive in holding a position that would give them access to a roped-off room, and a deep hurt and resentment from others who felt unwanted and unwelcome by those behind the closed doors.

Over one thousand comments came through in less than twenty-four hours as well as hundreds of direct messages with comments ranging from those who didn't even know what a greenroom was to rage and threats.

> *"Where are we supposed to go to decompress after leading worship?"*
> *"I just get so overstimulated by all the people ... I'm an introvert."*
> *"Performing takes a different presence of mind than caring for children in a nursery ..."*
> *"You could use your platform for better purposes ..."*

In a time when the enemy has come in through the back door and blown down our house, stolen precious lives and ministries, and divided the people of God in unprecedented ways, all many Christians could do was defend their precious greenrooms. Other comments came in, such as:

> *"It always feels so elite, like a room only for the special*
> *people."*
> *"I've been kicked out of greenrooms because I wasn't*
> *part of the team."*
> *"I work in the nursery and we don't get a break.*
> *Shoot, we don't need a greenroom, we need an*
> *escape room."*

Our churches should never be a place to reinforce elitism by position or title, offering rest and rejuvenation to some and leaving others working equally as hard to fend for themselves. We are all servants in the House of God, regardless of visibility or proximity to those we serve.

It is vital as individuals serving our local churches, as leaders in God's Church, we understand this Kingdom principle that the last shall be first and first shall be last, but also the last part of that scripture, "for many be called, but few chosen" (Matt. 20:16 KJV). We don't come to be served, we come to serve and not everyone will be equipped emotionally to live a sacrificial life, for it isn't by our own strength any of us are able to remain standing, but only by the power and authority of our Almighty God. So when we attempt to do it on our own, under our own name, fame, or influence, when idols like greenrooms are confronted, we lash out. We fear being irrelevant, we fear being orphaned more than we fear the Lord.

Until we call it out and gently remind one another we have a good Father who owns the cattle on a thousand hills and stop feeding our spoiled selves, we will remain in bondage to this spirit. We have a Father. Nobody has been left behind. We all have a seat at his table. Nobody is getting more than you, and if they are, it's their responsibility to steward what they have been given and they will be held accountable by God and God alone.

There are no orphans in the Kingdom of God, only sons and daughters.

As I learn more about the orphan spirit, I ask myself, *Will we ever truly believe we belong and are wanted?* Even though I know who I am and Whose I am, the enemy is quick to remind me what I lack. I still fear being rejected; I want people to like me. I find myself wanting to belong and fit in. I don't want to be irrelevant or forgotten. I do get jealous sometimes. I have been manipulative. I have rejected wise counsel, believing I know best.

> **There are no orphans in the Kingdom of God, only sons and daughters.**

It is possible to be surrounded by family and still believe we have nothing or no one.

How we treat one another either legitimizes these orphan-spirit lies or exposes them. If we create a place that competes and compares much like the world does, we aren't truly set apart as a city on a hill.

A Royal Adoption

As I minister in churches big and small of all denominations and backgrounds, I am encouraged. Yes, pastors are weary and congregants leery, but I'm watching churches wake up and begin the difficult process of biblical renewal using foundational building blocks. There was an innocence to the early Church in its infancy. Though still imperfect humans carrying a perfect Gospel, there was an undeniable unity among them.

In Acts 2:42 it says that the people were devoted to:

- the apostles' teachings
- fellowship
- sharing meals
- prayer

This was the posture of the people on Pentecost as the Holy Spirit moved and dwelled among them. It's the picture of what Sunday morning could look like in our churches for each of us if we were intentional in welcoming spiritual orphans home into a safe place.

- We preach the Word of God.
- We fellowship through worship, volunteering, conversations in foyers, and hugs between services.
- We break bread together in church through Communion and beyond church walls in one another's homes and restaurants.
- We make prayer a priority, not an afterthought.

When I've been hurt or disappointed by Christians in my past, my first instinct was to look for a community of people to commiserate with me and validate my status as an outcast. Unfortunately, I didn't have to look too far because those communities are loud and robust, and the world is a willing recipient of those rejected by our churches. What I really needed were people who would help me heal and remind me who I was as a daughter of God. I needed those who would take me to Jesus, not further from him.

We are all called to be Upper Room friends.

I want friends who will lower me through a roof to my healing, who will worship with me when I'm in bondage, friends who run to Jesus on my behalf, who will call me out of my pity party of an early grave. I want that Upper Room community who isn't afraid of a little fire, who knows how to fan a flame and stir up a gift. I need intercessors who will go to war without ceasing and worshippers who will go to battle as warriors. I want a Church who knows the Word of God and wields it like a double-edged sword, for it is burning in their bellies, burning in their bones. I want an army who knows how to fight and a family who knows how to love.

There will be counterfeit communities and families who will promise you solidarity but leave you in solitude. They will promise healing only to lick your wounds with their saltiness. They will offer sweet revenge but it's a cup of bitterness. Don't forget this: misery loves company so don't pull up a chair until you know who else is at the table. Be wise of where you sit, aware of who invited you, and discern if you'll be pulled down to a lower standard or called up to a higher purpose.

The longer our churches allow those who lead from fear, insecurity, and competition to hold titles, positions, and platforms, the more we risk losing those truly Fatherless coming through our front doors each week. Our church building should be the safest place on our entire planet. Let's behave like the royal priesthood that we are, the chosen generation, a peculiar people who look and act different from the world.

Through community, fellowship, prayer, and God's Word, we can rewrite our story and help others do the same from one of abandonment and rejection to a story of adoption and restoration.

It's a hard knock life in this upside-down kingdom.

But we have a good Father and each other.

We have a Home.

Reflection Prayer

"I confess I sometimes feel like I don't fit in. I often feel jealous when I see others getting what looks like more than me and I wonder if you see me. I want to remember that as your child, I have been given a beautiful inheritance that cannot be taken. Help me rest in the truth that you love me, you are proud of me, and you will never leave me or abandon me. Help me be a welcoming presence wherever I go. May I make others feel loved and heard, and for those looking for a friend, help me be one and also point them to you. Thank you for adopting me into your family and being my Heavenly Father."

Chapter 4

WHEN WOLVES WEAR WOOL

"So guard yourselves and God's people. Feed and shepherd God's flock—his church, purchased with his own blood—over which the Holy Spirit has appointed you as leaders. I know that false teachers, like vicious wolves, will come in among you after I leave, not sparing the flock. Even some men from your own group will rise up and distort the truth in order to draw a following."

Acts 20:28–30

The woods were particularly haunting, casting ominous shadows of yellow and green as the sun filtered through dew-soaked trees. I cautiously made my way down the trail toward a clearing. Nothing looked familiar, had I been here before?

I heard twigs snapping to my left and I knew I wasn't alone. The sky was growing darker and I quickened my footsteps as rustling sounds in the bushes grew closer to me. Was it a bear? A mountain lion? A giant elk preparing to charge?

"Baaaaaa ..."

Sheep? I stopped dead in my tracks as the bleating became louder and sheep slowly emerged from the woods, hundreds of them, looking at me with big eyes under bushy wool. They were precious, their snow-white coats like a freshly fallen winter among the spring evergreens. Yet I couldn't help but notice they looked nervous, almost antsy with each tender step toward the path.

Something wasn't right. They seemed frightened, and I, too, felt afraid, my heart pounding with familiar discernment that an enemy was close by. Birds chirping, the wind whispering, I began scouring the tree line as their bleating grew louder and louder until something strange caught my eye.

There was a sheep crouched under a large tree, head down, hiding in plain sight. I began walking toward the creature, and as I got closer, it slowly lifted its nose to expose a long snout, yellow eyes, and large fangs under a pelt of sheepskin. It didn't growl or do anything to give away its identity, rather it locked eyes with me and wouldn't let go. It knew I had seen it for what it was, and now I was its prey.

I started to run away, to run for my life, but it didn't pursue me.

I wasn't who it wanted.

That wolf was after the entire flock.

Counting Wolves

I woke up with my heart pounding and sweat dripping down my back, the image of that wolf so masterfully camouflaged among all those innocent sheep seared into my brain. My bedroom was still dark; I couldn't help but wonder why these spiritually charged dreams always seemed to wake me at the scariest part of the night.

As I caught my breath, I lay back down and stared up at the ceiling afraid to go back to sleep, lest the Lord send me back into those woods to make his final points.

I didn't need a dream interpreter to tell me what it all meant. At thirty-two years old I had spent the last few years under multiple pastors, leaders, and organizations and had seen all I needed to understand what the Holy Spirit was trying to tell me through that dream.

Wolves in sheep's clothing were hiding in plain sight, positioned among the people of God and intent on devouring his sheep. Their ultimate desire is to steal, kill, and destroy those who follow the Great Shepherd. When the enemy gains access to the flock due to negligent shepherds who haven't safeguarded their field, it is open season on the vulnerable.

God has much to say regarding shepherds who aren't protecting their sheep. Read with me the words God spoke to Ezekiel:

> Tell those shepherds, "GOD, the Master, says: Doom to you shepherds of Israel, feeding your own mouths! Aren't shepherds supposed to feed sheep? You drink the milk, you make clothes from the wool, you roast the lambs, but you don't feed the sheep. You don't build up the weak ones, don't heal the sick, don't doctor the injured, don't go after the strays, don't look for the lost. You bully and badger them. And now they're scattered every which way because there was no shepherd—scattered and easy pickings for wolves and coyotes. Scattered—*my sheep!*—exposed and vulnerable across mountains

and hills. My sheep scattered all over the world, and

no one out looking for them!" (Ezek. 34:1–6 MSG)

The sheep of the house are scattered and there is an enemy among us.

In 1 Peter 5:8–9 we read the warning: "Stay alert! Watch out for your great enemy, the devil. He prowls around like a roaring lion, looking for someone to devour. Stand firm against him, and be strong in your faith. Remember that your family of believers all over the world is going through the same kind of suffering you are."

Personally, I knew this dream was a warning from the Lord regarding a church where I was an interim worship pastor at the time. There was a woman in an executive position who craved authority and status and she was doing everything in her power to eliminate anyone in her path who questioned her leadership. I had stepped into the role temporarily while their staffed worship pastor took his sabbatical, however, he chose not to return, and I was on staff indefinitely under her watchful eye. Every time I tried to voice concern regarding this leader, I was told I was the problem. I felt helpless to protect the other staff members and congregants.

I didn't go back to sleep that night; I lay in bed until sunrise thinking of every wolf I had seen in my lifetime as a pastor's kid and in ministry. It was unsettling how many went undetected, and for so long, and I was shocked by how many were still in high levels of leadership, continuing to abuse the sheep without any repercussions. As churchgoers, we learn to live among them, walking tenderly to not upset one of these impostors in fear that exposing them might sacrifice the lives of the innocent.

What we don't realize is we lose more sheep by tiptoeing around the disguised wolves than we would by taking the risk to bring them into the light. Looking back, I realize that our church staff members don't always feel equipped to confront these wolves, and they would rather quit than risk their own lives fighting something everyone else is choosing to ignore.

Sheep Are Not Beasts of Burden

Unlike the donkey or the ox, sheep are not meant to carry heavy loads. Our Great Shepherd knew this about us, his own sheep, which is why I believe Jesus said, "Come to me, all you who are weary and burdened, and I will give you rest. Take my yoke upon you and learn from me, for I am gentle and humble in heart, and you will find rest for your souls. For my yoke is easy and my burden is light" (Matt. 11:28–30 NIV).

I also believe it's why we read in Hebrews 12:1, "Let us strip off every weight that slows us down, especially the sin that so easily trips us up."

We aren't meant to be beasts of burden and yet we carry so much weight in this world. We are holding on to

> We lose more sheep by tiptoeing around the disguised wolves than we would by taking the risk to bring them into the light.

offense, fear, anxiety, and so much more simply by being human. Our churches should be the one place we sheep can gather to unload some of our weight, yet it seems as if even more is added to our load there.

Church staff are no longer predominantly raised in the church or arriving with a seminary background. As a church leader, you may be hiring brand-new Christ followers, and this may be their first time working among Christians or serving in a church. Many of them come in with big expectations based on assumptions they've made about working in a church. Many are young, it's their first job, and they may have spent their early twenties in church ministry programs rather than formal university. Others come in wide eyed and naive with dreams of being the next big worship leader or world-traveling evangelist.

Like the sheep in my dream, these staff members or volunteers are purehearted, innocent, and completely oblivious that an enemy is among them. Then one day, without warning, the wolf's true nature emerges. Perhaps through narcissistic leadership, abuse, manipulation, intimidation, or subtle toxic management strategy, the innocent sheep are exposed to the wolf hiding in plain sight. The weight of the disappointment, betrayal, and frustration is too much for many of our staff and they would rather quit than contend for a healthy culture.

Are you wondering why your staff culture is dismal and good people keep leaving?

- They are afraid of being fired or reprimanded for questioning issues observed in leadership.
- They have been labeled gossips or divisive in the past for reporting anything negative against leadership.

- They have risked properly reporting abuse or inappropriate behavior to HR without any results.
- They have seen that accountability and repercussions will vary depending on who it is and their title.
- The church board or elders aren't informed of matters involving the senior pastor, his team, or others high in leadership.
- They have watched their peers lose positions, platform, or respect for addressing difficult situations.
- They have seen abusers promoted and talent trump character.
- They have grown weary of yelling "fire!" when nobody wants to acknowledge the smoke.

As I've interviewed those in the Raised to Stay community, I've uncovered a consistent theme among veteran and novice church staff: there are wolves in sheep's clothing terrorizing the people of God, and in many cases, it's a high-level leader or even the senior pastor. Because of their status and position, it feels impossible that anything will be done to investigate allegations of abuse or poor leadership, leaving those in lower positions of power with two options: quit or be fired.

Pastors tell me they want to know what is happening under their roof. It saddens them when they find out their staff doesn't feel safe or believe their voices are valued. But it baffles me how few senior pastors actually know their staff due to insulating themselves, and it's only getting worse as churches get bigger and more campus locations are added. Senior leaders heavily rely on team leads and other high-level leaders to mentor and disciple newer employees. But that means the pastor must have a good understanding of who is shepherding their staff.

The solution is for pastors, elders, and senior leaders to listen to their staff—those who are in trenches they can't see, with people they don't know, in conversations they can't hear. Leaders with the power to make change would learn so much by taking their people to lunch, assuring them they are safe, their words confidential, and their hearts trusted. If you're a leader, ask your staff permission to go deep into difficult questions even if you're afraid their response might be hard to receive. We can show them we are a safe place, and even after they use their voice in hard conversations, we can maintain a healthy relationship that doesn't bring shame to them for using it.

Proper structure in place will keep wolves out of our field and expose them if they get in, and we cannot punish the sheep who are trying to expose wolves.

Pastors, listen to your staff. Elders, know who you have appointed to protect the sheep. Leaders, remember that being feared isn't the same as being respected.

The Rock Ram

During my time as an interim worship pastor, I learned a lot about what to do when you encounter a wolf in sheep's clothing. As a younger leader (with a high justice streak), I lacked discernment to know when to quietly pray in my position as a watchman on the wall and when to confront the enemy head-on. I was impulsive, loud, unwise at times. I was scared.

When I think back to my dream, the wolf knew I had seen it. It wasn't afraid of me; it didn't even try to hide. There was a pride in that wolf that knew even if I chose to expose it as an impostor, the rest of the sheep would rather run back into the trees than fight it and I would be left alone on the dark path to fend for myself.

I was tired of fighting alone.

One Sunday morning as I was clearing bulletins from the pews after service, a gentleman whom I had never seen before was waiting for me at the back of the sanctuary. He introduced himself and asked if he could give me a word of encouragement. I was desperate for someone to acknowledge how difficult this season had been; even if it was to rebuke me, I just wanted someone to say something to validate what I was discerning.

This man, whom I never saw again, sat me down and said, "Young lady, you are a ram among sheep. Unlike sheep who are gentle and easily led by whomever holds a staff, a ram has power to penetrate, and I see you as a ram in the family of God. You move with confidence to the front of the pack, and when there is an obstacle that keeps the sheep from moving forward, you butt your head against those rocks until a tiny pinhole appears, but you must stop trying to break down the entire wall. It's not your job. Once that pinhole of light appears, it's up to the rest of the sheep to knock it down to their freedom. Don't stop butting your head up against the rocks, the sheep depend on your power to start their path to freedom."

Growing up, I had received a lot of well-meaning encouragement from people, and I was taught to weigh their words wisely. If it didn't align with the Word of God, if it didn't match with the words of Jesus or the heart of the Father, I was careful to spit out the bones and hold on to the meat. This word of encouragement in particular left me speechless in the empty sanctuary. I had felt so alone in this fight, like the loud kid always sent to the principal's office. I always thought I was the problem. Why couldn't I be like everyone else and just blindly go with the flow? Why was I always seeing the problems and flaws?

I love the psalmist David's words in Psalm 144:1, "Praise the LORD, who is my rock. He trains my hands for war and gives my fingers skill for battle."

God trusted me. He trusts you. God has given us a strategy for war against a very strategic enemy, and he has trained our hands to fight and overcome an enemy with a very weak battle plan. These wolves, though they look like flesh and blood, are an evil attempt of Satan to divide the family of God. Fighting the spirit of darkness looks different than exposing a person; we fight differently.

We fight with weapons of intercession, worship, wise counsel, and humility. We don't panic, we prophesy, and we remain in position with the safety of the sheep as our main priority, not our reputations or personal agendas. In my dream, the enemy wanted me to think I was the problem because he knew I saw him, and he needed me out of the way. And he knows that once Jesus is in the picture, the enemy can't touch the Lord's sheep.

Dear Rock Rams, you aren't the problem, you are the prophetic messengers called to care for the people of God. I know you might have headaches from hitting your heads up against the same walls, but don't grow weary in your mission.

Shepherds Needed

I remember a time I was called into my supervisor's office to discuss another staff member. I had spent a year under this woman who made it clear in every one-on-one that she had the power to fire me, and I should be grateful she chose to keep me around. In this meeting she wanted me to tell her everything I knew about my peer and pressed me for information until it felt as if I was exaggerating details just to get out of her office. As we wrapped up the meeting, she handed me a folder and said, "As my associate pastor, I expect you to address the concerning behavior and document everything. I'm giving you two hours."

My insides quaking, I knew I didn't have a choice. I went to their office, fumbled my way through an awkward and confusing confrontation, and went home sick to my stomach. I found out a couple of years later that the next day, my supervisor went to that person she had me reprimand and told them, "I heard Natalie came and talked with you yesterday, I'm so sorry she did that to you. You know how judgmental Natalie can be ..."

Turns out this tactic is commonly employed in structures where power dynamics are involved. It wouldn't be the only example in my life where a leader used their power and position to manipulate me, and I have learned through the Raised to Stay community that unfortunately many in our churches and Christian organizations have had similar experiences. The problem is it's hard to recognize in the moment and even harder to do anything about it if you do. It can look like pulling us into their confidence, gathering intel by "confidentially" asking us to share our opinions on people or situations, only to later call us divisive or gossips and remove us from a position to make room for other talented, more accommodating staff.

Perhaps you have been visited by holy henchmen (like me)—high-level staff members and leaders who do the things another leader doesn't want to do—and when they speak, their words are not their own but an unreliable interpretation of what has been communicated to them behind closed doors.

In our personal desires for validation and affirmation, which can then grow to want authority and power, it is tempting to dedicate our service to protecting some at the expense of many, hoping our loyalty will somehow gain us opportunity or favor. It can feel noble and for a greater cause, but how quickly we become pawns in this game of chess, how quickly we take the Turkish Delight only to find ourselves imprisoned by the very ones who promised us a Kingdom.

In the book *The Lion, the Witch and the Wardrobe*, C. S. Lewis writes:

> At last the Turkish Delight was all finished and Edmund was looking very hard at the empty box and wishing that she would ask him whether he would like some more. Probably the Queen knew quite well what he was thinking; for she knew, though Edmund did not, that this was enchanted Turkish Delight and that anyone who had once tasted it would want more and more of it, and would even, if they were allowed, go on eating it till they killed themselves.[4]

It shouldn't surprise us when wolves find their way into our churches with as little security we have at our front doors. With everyone distracted by programming and publicity, nobody is protecting the sheep inside our church walls.

We forgot that as shepherds, we are called to love, protect, and feed God's sheep.

And who are the shepherds? The answer may surprise you.

The shepherds are you and me.

We have all been given a field to watch over in the form of our community, family, church family, neighborhood, workplace, and school, and sheep entrusted to us who live among us. We know the names and the needs, and we don't need the title of pastor to protect and serve the sheep around us.

> **The shepherds are you and me.**

When we see something happening in our church that is harming God's sheep, we should feel full freedom and permission to take our concerns to elders or human resource departments with confidence they will do whatever they can to thoroughly investigate.

But there are often repercussions when healthy shepherds see the wolves and finally have the courage to report harmful, abusive behavior. I cannot tell you how many times I have followed the guidance of Matthew 18 (Jesus' model of how to handle personal conflict) to express concern about a leader who is hurting me or another staff member, only to be told by the church board or an elder, "They aren't trying to hurt anyone, they are just protecting the organization."

How do we good, intended shepherds know when to risk our own reputations and even our positions for the good of the sheep?

In the book of Esther we meet Queen Esther, who learned the lives of her Jewish people were in danger at the hands of the wicked Haman. Knowing she was placed in the palace at that time for great purpose, Esther had to use discernment and wisdom to know how and when to approach the king. Her story offers us a blueprint for how we might prayerfully consider confronting people and situations that threaten the emotional, spiritual, and often physical well-being of the sheep.

She knew going to the king could cost her life, as it was the law that nobody approached the king without an invitation. So she told her cousin Mordecai, "Go and gather together all the Jews of Susa and fast for me. Do not eat or drink for three days, night or day. My maids and I will do the same. And then, though it is against the law, I will go in to see the king. If I must die, I must die" (Est. 4:16).

- Esther gathered her community.
- Esther fasted.
- Esther prayed.
- Esther was willing to die for her people.

When we see people being harmed, it is normal to react out of emotion or desire to see justice. Queen Esther demonstrates true meekness, or power under control, using both her position and the spiritual practice of fasting to expose evil. I love how Esther asked the Jews of Susa to fast for her; she knew to help others she would need an army surrounding her.

Much like we are instructed on airplanes to secure our own oxygen masks first before helping others, we cannot forget that God has given us tools such as prayer, fasting, and wise counsel to help us. We should seek guidance for ourselves and be strengthened and solid with the truth before we'll be equipped to lead others out of seemingly impossible situations.

When people ask me where change in our churches can begin, I always say it starts with me. It's important for us to get healthy ourselves before we can contribute to creating a healthy church culture. Here are some steps to getting healthy and holding a right perspective with God:

- Address any need for validation or affirmation by mere mortals. Colossians 3:23–24 says, "Work willingly at whatever you do, as though you were working for the Lord rather than for people. Remember that the Lord will give you an inheritance as your reward, and that the Master you are serving is Christ."
- Wait on our God-appointed assignments.
- Seek positions that don't require promotion from man or that demand anything in return.
- Refuse to take the dangling carrot or to fall for any promise to be collected for loyalty to a person or organization.
- As a leader, never be too busy to do hard things or to have hard conversations (in person—not in email or text). When we pull others in to plead our case or defend our position, we are causing more harm to

the sheep and often exposing our own weakness, not only as a leader, but as a child of God.

There are no ladders to climb in the Kingdom of God. We get ahead by being last, through living with integrity, discernment, and humility. We aren't called to be sidekicks who do an earthly master's bidding. We are leaders called to protect and love the sheep entrusted to us. We see this in John chapter 21 verse 17 in a conversation between Jesus and Peter.

> **There are no ladders to climb in the Kingdom of God. We get ahead by being last, through living with integrity, discernment, and humility.**

A third time he asked him, "Simon son of John, do you love me?"

Peter was hurt that Jesus asked the question a third time. He said, "Lord, you know everything. You know that I love you."

Jesus said, "Then feed my sheep."

Before Jesus left the earth, he wanted to make sure Peter wasn't focused on his failure of denying Jesus but on the mission before him: serving each soul who would cross his path. If Peter truly loved Jesus with all his heart, mind, and soul, he would feed the Lord's sheep.

Reflection Prayer

"Thank you, Jesus, for loving your sheep and pursuing the one who has gone astray. I have been that one at times. I want to be the kind of Christ follower who protects and loves your sheep. Help me to discern when to use my voice to defend and protect and when to intercede in situations where I see wolves in sheep's clothing. I ask you to expose those hiding in plain sight. Help me to forgive others who haven't protected and cared for me. Thank you for never taking your eyes off me."

PART 2

REBUILDING

JESUS, OUR FIRM FOUNDATION

*"For no one can lay any foundation other than
the one we already have—Jesus Christ."*

1 Corinthians 3:11

Chapter 5

A HOUSE BUILT ON THE HOLY SPIRIT

Fire and Fruit

"And everyone present was filled with the Holy Spirit and began speaking in other languages, as the Holy Spirit gave them this ability."

Acts 2:4

Simply talking about church hurt, spiritual abuse, and a desire for healthy church culture doesn't bring change. It's easy to dissect other leaders, criticize religious institutions and organizations, and tell stories of our past, but without actively pursuing the healing that comes with hard conversations, counseling, and confessing our own sins, we will remain sick and stuck.

As I was preparing messages for churches and conferences this year, I kept returning to the book of Acts. Although I have spent time in these passages, now it was as if I were reading the familiar stories and scriptures for the first time. I realized I was looking at a blueprint for a healthy church. Everything we need to start construction is right there; Acts emphasizes vital building blocks needed for the foundation of the church, including preaching, teaching, prayer, worship, and community. God through his Word has given us the foundation, framework, and floorplan to a church he can use for his glory in these last days. God has given us the tools; we just need to use them!

The book of Acts is a sequel to the Gospel of Luke, both written by Luke, a doctor who was partnering with Paul in his missionary journey. Following the four Gospels, this book shifts language from Kingdom conversation to a new organization and focus: the Church. In Acts 2, we find ourselves in the Upper Room on the day of Pentecost, with Luke describing the beautiful experience of the real-time birth of the Church before his eyes. Without the book of Acts, we would miss out on the remaining eleven disciples' journeys and the apostle Paul's work as they took the Gospel of Jesus Christ beyond Israel and to the world.

The Spirit-Filled Life

When the Holy Spirit came into the Upper Room, Luke described it as "a sound like a strong wind, gale force—no one could tell where it came from. It filled the whole building. Then, like a wildfire, the Holy Spirit spread through their ranks, and they started speaking in a number of different languages as the Spirit prompted them" (Acts 2:1–4 MSG).

To help break up Acts chapter 2 for better understanding, it can be divided into four sections:

1. **The Arrival of the Holy Spirit** (Acts 2:1–4)
2. **The Reaction to the Holy Spirit's Arrival**
   (Acts 2:5–13)
   a. Amazement (Acts 2:5–12)
   b. Mockery (Acts 2:13)
3. **The Explanation of the Holy Spirit's Arrival**
   (Acts 2:14–36)
4. **The Effect of the Holy Spirit's Arrival**
   (Acts 2:37–47)
   a. Conviction (Acts 2:37)
   b. Confession (Acts 2:38–41)
   c. Commencement of the Church
      (Acts 2:42–47)[5]

Can you imagine being in a church service and this is happening right before your eyes? This is happening *to* you! Those in the room at that moment were human and had very different reactions to what they were witnessing. Some were amazed, saying, "They're speaking our languages, describing God's mighty works!" and others mocked, "They're drunk on cheap wine."

Growing up as a teenager in the Pentecostal church, I remember personally experiencing these contrasting reactions. In a congregation of five hundred people, there were many who believed everything they were seeing and hearing, and others who thought the rest had gone crazy. Inviting a friend to Sunday church was risky because you never knew what might happen, and if they would still want to be your friend after. Some friends saw the power of God move in my church and wanted to come back, and others saw the same power on display and thought we were crazy. Their parents were on the phone with my parents the next night.

I have grown to love the Holy Spirit and how he moves among the people of God with such precision. The beautiful part about the Holy Spirit is that as part of the Trinity, he is always in alignment with the mission of God and Jesus: the Great Commission. He isn't out of control, scary, or out of order, and he doesn't go rogue. He moves in tandem with God the Father and God the Son, ministering with purpose and intentionality.

Though it may have appeared chaotic in the Upper Room, those who were speaking in unknown languages were speaking the native languages of many in the room, describing God's mighty works and bearing witness to the saving message of Jesus Christ for those who had yet to hear it. There was purpose in this outpouring because God is a God of order.

Peter responded immediately by explaining there was no way those speaking in tongues were drunk; after all, it was only nine o'clock in the morning. He was quick to remind them of the words of the prophet Joel who wrote of these things that were to come.

> "In the Last Days," God says,
> "I will pour out my Spirit
>   on every kind of people:
> Your sons will prophesy,
>   also your daughters;
> Your young men will see visions,
>   your old men dream dreams.

When the time comes,

    I'll pour out my Spirit

On those who serve me, men and women both,

    and they'll prophesy." (Acts 2:17–18 MSG)

Everything that happened in the Upper Room through the Holy Spirit was in alignment with the scriptures, even if some people couldn't understand what they were witnessing. Peter took the opportunity to explain through teaching and led the first church into repentance, salvation, and eventually evangelism to spread the message of Jesus Christ.

There are a lot of movements and books that tell us our lives are purpose-driven, and though it's true, we cannot forget our original God-given purpose is to be Spirit-filled and Spirit-led. If my purpose makes me competitive, combative, hard to lead, and divisive, I am not truly being led by the Holy Spirit. The Spirit-filled life prefers others, serves others, or puts our personal preferences in the back seat to what is best for the sheep, seeking the voice of God above all other voices in our lives.

When the Holy Spirit fell on those in the Upper Room,

> **If my purpose makes me competitive, combative, hard to lead, and divisive, I am not truly being led by the Holy Spirit.**

it was with great purpose, even if not everyone could understand that purpose in the moment. Your Spirit-filled life has great purpose because it is Spirit-led, and God wants to fill you up with his **love**, **joy**, **peace**, **patience**, **kindness**, **goodness**, **faithfulness**, **gentleness**, and **self-control** to show others his power and glory, not our own.

The Promise

Prior to the Holy Spirit coming into the Upper Room, we find very anxious disciples asking Jesus a lot of questions prior to his final ascent into heaven. In Acts 1:6 they asked, "Lord, has the time come for you to free Israel and restore our kingdom?" Jesus was firm in his response, saying, "The Father alone has the authority to set those dates and times, and they are not for you to know. *But you will receive power when the Holy Spirit comes upon you.* And you will be my witnesses, telling people about me everywhere—in Jerusalem, throughout Judea, in Samaria, and to the ends of the earth" (Acts 1:7–8).

In these verses Jesus was letting everyone within the sound of his voice know that even though they didn't have the answers they wanted or a detailed plan to do what he was asking—taking the Gospel to the ends of the earth—he would leave with them the Holy Spirit as they went on mission.

But what did that even mean? I'm sure the disciples genuinely wondered this themselves.

After they had physically walked with Jesus on the earth, I'm sure they couldn't wrap their human minds around him leaving them. Yet just as the Old Testament prophets had used the promise of a coming Messiah to comfort the Church, Jesus would now comfort his disciples with the promise of the Holy Spirit that would never leave them.

In John 14:26, Jesus told the disciples, "But when the Father sends the Advocate as my representative—that is, the Holy Spirit—he will teach you everything and will remind you of everything I have told you." The Amplified Bible says it like this:

> But the Comforter (Counselor, Helper, Intercessor, Advocate, Strengthener, Standby), the Holy Spirit, Whom the Father will send in My name [in My place, to represent Me and act on My behalf], He will teach you all things. And He will cause you to recall (will remind you of, bring to your remembrance) everything I have told you. (AMPC)

The Holy Spirit Jesus promised the disciples is the same Holy Spirit he promises us today as we share the message of Jesus Christ to a lost world.

The Holy Spirit is our:

- Comforter
- Counselor
- Helper
- Intercessor
- Advocate
- Strengthener
- Standby

When we say yes to being a disciple and picking up our cross to follow him, we are filled with the Holy Spirit. While many Christians are quick to focus on the gifts that come from the filling of the Holy Spirit as outlined in the scriptures in 1 Corinthians 12:7–10 and Ephesians 4:11 (administration, discernment, evangelism, exhortation, faith, giving, healing, hospitality, knowledge, leadership, mercy, prophecy, serving, speaking in tongues, teaching, wisdom), we are also given the fruits of the Holy Spirit.

Galatians 5:22–25 tells us what to look for in our lives as we ask to be filled with the Holy Spirit:

> But the Holy Spirit produces this kind of fruit in our lives: *love, joy, peace, patience, kindness, goodness, faithfulness, gentleness, and self-control.* There is no law against these things!
>
> Those who belong to Christ Jesus have nailed the passions and desires of their sinful nature to his cross and crucified them there. Since we are living by the Spirit, let us follow the Spirit's leading in every part of our lives.

This world doesn't care how many gifts of the Spirit we have if the fruit we bear is rotten.

The apostle Paul says it even better, "Though I speak with the tongues of men and of angels, but have not love, I have become sounding brass or a clanging cymbal. And though I have the gift of prophecy, and understand all mysteries and all knowledge, and though I have all faith, so that I could remove mountains, but have not love, I am nothing" (1 Cor. 13:1–2 NKJV).

Those we live and work among daily are watching our lives and looking for the fruit. They are looking for love. They are wondering if we have joy in hard seasons of loss and disappointment and, if so, where we get it. They can't understand how we can have peace that passes all understanding in the chaos of the world. Where does this kindness and goodness come from? When everyone else seems hardened, how have we remained gentle and meek and purehearted?

Every word that comes from my mouth should be full of the Spirit of God. I should be planting seeds of hope, words of life.

> Every word that comes from my mouth should be full of the Spirit of God. I should be planting seeds of hope, words of life.

Are we the same Spirit-filled Christians offstage as we are on the platform?

The Proof Is in the Fruit

I carry a core memory from my senior year in high school that still haunts me to this day. I had been with many of my friends since kindergarten; they knew and loved me as the pastor's kid with a curfew and clean mouth. On this particular day, surrounded by football players in jerseys, my cheer team, and others who were more like cousins than classmates, I did something unprecedented.

While their volume grew with the ornery banter of jocks, curse words flying overhead and laughter deepening, as if in a slow-motion '90s rom-com scene, I said a word that had never come out of my mouth. I regretted it the moment I heard the foul rhetoric leave my lips, but it was too late. The entire table went silent; picture a record player scratching our entire scene to a halt, just like in *Saved by the Bell*, Zack Morris–style, with a "Time out" for cinematic flair.

Every head jerked my direction, eyes wide as the girl who rarely said "crap" had just used its forbidden counterpart. My best friend looked at me in horror as she placed her hand on my arm.

"Natalie! Why would you say *that* word?!"

Their response to the Christian girl saying one curse word might feel a bit extreme these days, as I've heard worse words on Sunday mornings from Christians in greenrooms, but it changed me.

I realized that even though many of them didn't have a relationship with Jesus, and though they made fun of me at times and thought I acted holier than thou, the consistency of my faith and the way I spoke offered them a strange comfort and stability.

They didn't like the rotten fruit I displayed that afternoon because as hard as I tried to be like them, we all knew I was different. Not just because my dad was a pastor, not just because I didn't party or say bad words, but because when everything in our teenage world was chaotic and off kilter, I was the one voice who offered a bit of stability and consistency.

My Spirit-filled life produced fruit they had not yet tasted.

The moment we say yes to Jesus, we are filled with the Holy Spirit. We don't have to earn it or beg for it; the Holy Spirit is a gift to every believer who calls Jesus their Lord and Savior. In John 15, Jesus uses the image of a vine and branch to explain the relationship between us and God.

He says in John 15:4–5, "Remain in me, and I will remain in you. For a branch cannot produce fruit if it is severed from the vine, and you cannot be fruitful unless you remain in me. Yes, I am the vine; you are the branches. Those who remain in me, and I in them, will produce much fruit. For apart from me you can do nothing."

How do we know if we're filled with the Holy Spirit? We see proof in our fruit.

There will be days we feel the tangible presence of God, and other days we need to trust he is still with us in what feels like his silence. But we will have the fruit from past seasons of obedience to the Spirit.

Am I loving, joyful, patient, kind, good to others, faithful, gentle, and operating in self-control? Or am I hateful, full of anxiety, impatient, unkind, mean to others, unreliable, harsh, and living in self-preservation?

The Holy Spirit will work as a guide to expose our sin, convict us of areas we are falling short, and put us back on mission, if we remain connected to the vine no matter the storms threatening to pull us off the lifeline. Jesus continues this message to his disciples, taking the imagery a step further:

> But if you remain in me and my words remain in
> you, you may ask for anything you want, and it will

be granted! When you produce much fruit, you
are my true disciples. This brings great glory to my
Father. (John 15:7–8)

True disciples produce much fruit.

I am sure the apostles were asking a lot of questions as the
church was growing daily. Can you imagine pioneering something
so new that was growing so quickly? They most likely had a few days
they wanted to quit, which is why they had to delegate. Luke tells us:

> But as the believers rapidly multiplied, there were
> rumblings of discontent. The Greek-speaking
> believers complained about the Hebrew-speaking
> believers, saying that their widows were being
> discriminated against in the daily distribution of
> food.
>
> So the Twelve called a meeting of all the
> believers. They said, "We apostles should spend
> our time teaching the word of God, not running a
> food program. And so, brothers, select seven men
> who are well respected and are full of the Spirit
> and wisdom. We will give them this responsibility.
> Then we apostles can spend our time in prayer and
> teaching the word." (Acts 6:1–4)

The apostles were looking for leaders, builders, planters, co-
laborers who were well respected, full of the Spirit, and wise.

When looking within our own church walls, it is important to search for signs of a Spirit-filled church. A Spirit-filled church will be a purpose-filled church because it will be on mission with the message of Jesus Christ as well as respected, full of the Spirit, and wise.

What are some qualities we should see in our Spirit-filled churches?

- Preaches the Bible as Gospel truth, from Genesis to Revelation, leaving nothing out and not adding their own opinions or agendas.
- Worships in Spirit and in truth, singing psalms and hymns that point others to Jesus and his character and attributes.
- Serves their church family and surrounding community to meet the needs of the lost and hurting through discipleship, mentorship, and Great Commission–minded ministry.
- Provides community to those searching for family and connection in a variety of ways: children's ministry, youth, young adults, women's ministry, men's ministry, widows, the grieving, the addict, the single parent, etc.
- Confronts conflict at a congregant and staff level with consistent biblical processes such as in Matthew 18, following through each step to bring unity and reconciliation.

- Holds leaders accountable, from the pulpit to the pew, and protects the sheep before protecting personalities or reputations.
- Confesses sin, admits shortcomings, repents, reconciles, and models true sorrow before the congregation and staff.

As we can see from the first four chapters of this book, we have been building our churches on a lot of things outside the Holy Spirit. Thank you, Jesus, for your grace and mercy for each of us!

Even when we have depended on our own talents, strengths, and reputations, or focused on building a brand rather than building the church God has asked us to build, Jesus has still extended an invitation to us to build alongside him.

And it's here in this place of partnership with the Holy Spirit we see both the fire and the fruit provided for us to accomplish the work set out before us.

A Fruitful Foundation

I have had the honor of serving on many church staff teams who have taught me more than I could have ever taught them. I left better because that is what happens when we're Spirit-led, we become even more Spirit-filled, even in the seasons we thought would kill us.

God loves to turn what we thought was our crucifixion into our resurrection.

The Spirit-filled Church always leaves people better than when they arrived.

As I visit churches today and speak to leaders, I am encouraged more than ever that God is laying a fruitful foundation through this generation. Yes, there are still churches pushing celebrity culture and catering to Christian consumers. Yes, there are still many of us struggling with an orphan spirit and wolves in sheep's clothing, but God is exposing the cracks and new foundations are being poured. He is so good he will use our broken pieces and past mistakes to build something beautiful.

I see a people who want revival more than we want revenge. We want to see the Kingdom of God come on earth as it is in heaven, and I see more of the good than I see the bad or unhealthy. I see leaders rising to the occasion and congregations unified like never before because they are desperate for more of God, desperate for a move of the Holy Spirit like those waiting for the promise of God to arrive in that Upper Room.

While in California I had the opportunity to preach at a decent-sized church in Modesto. I say "decent-sized" because the pastor and his wife were incredibly connected to their congregation, and I was amazed at their ability to remember names, children's names, situations, and health needs of those they intersected with over the course of the weekend.

> I see a people who want revival more than we want revenge.

"How did the procedure go, Jim?" "How is your daughter feeling, Margaret?" "We were praying for your exam all week, Amy."

They would turn to me and tell me the most intricate stories of those milling about their sanctuary. They cited dates and times of the milestone moments that led each new believer through their church doors and to become an active member and volunteer. Some were men who arrived by bus from a local halfway house and served in a variety of ways on Sunday mornings, many now clean and sober and active in the church family.

That Sunday morning as I preached through Acts 16 and the radical interruption that put Paul and Silas in a prison cell, I felt the Holy Spirit lead me in a different direction than I had planned. I asked the congregation, "How many of you have been impacted by your pastor's willingness to be radically interrupted for you?"

I watched as nearly half the room raised tattooed arms, their heads dropping as tears fell with gratitude. I then asked each one of them to come to the front of the sanctuary until I was staring out over empty chairs. The pastor and his wife stood in disbelief.

The proof was in their fruit.

They had laid a foundation that wasn't just thriving, it was multiplying.

The world won't know we are his disciples by our big buildings, fancy programs, or robust budgets. They won't know we are his disciples by our politics and hot takes. They will know we are his disciples by our great love for one another and the undeniable fruit in our lives and ministries.

Some of us are wondering why our ministries aren't growing; it's because we're mean.

People know good fruit from rotten apples.

It's time for the Church to inspect our fruit.

Paul writes in Ephesians 2:19–22:

> So now you Gentiles are no longer strangers and foreigners. You are citizens along with all of God's holy people. You are members of God's family. Together, we are his house, built on the foundation of the apostles and the prophets. And the cornerstone is Christ Jesus himself. We are carefully joined together in him, becoming a holy temple for the Lord. Through him you Gentiles are also being made part of this dwelling where God lives by his Spirit.

We are a dwelling place where God lives by his Spirit.
We have this same promise of the Holy Spirit.
He is our firm foundation.

Reflection Prayer

"Thank you, Jesus, for the promise of the Holy Spirit that rests upon me even now just as it did in the Upper Room. I want to be filled with your Holy Spirit and bear the fruits of the Spirit so that on days it feels impossible to love people and fulfill the Great Commission, I have strength to persevere because you are with me. Holy Spirit, come into my life, into your Church, fill us until we are overflowing with your power and love."

Chapter 6

A HOUSE BUILT ON MISSION

Revival and Resistance

*"But you will receive power when the
Holy Spirit comes upon you. And you will
be my witnesses, telling people about me
everywhere—in Jerusalem, throughout Judea,
in Samaria, and to the ends of the earth."*

Acts 1:8

The disciples were already asking Jesus some pretty serious questions
following the resurrection.

*You want us to do what? You want us to go where? Without you?
How? When?*

Let the disciples be an example to us all that we can physically
lose a leader and remain on mission.

I have sat through one too many "all church" meetings follow-ing the resignation or unfortunate firing of a senior pastor where everyone is looking at one another wide eyed and lost.

Leadership will constantly change; the wheel of favor never stops turning. But God and his mission to see lost people found through the Great Commandment and Great Commission have never changed. Even when we lose a leader, even when every board member walks, even when the entire staff is let go to make room for new staff, our mission remains the same. Yet these changes bring church splits, division among the family of God, hard feelings, and offense because the enemy will use anything he can to stop God's Church from growing.

And the disciples were so much like you and me, sitting wide eyed and staring at each other in disbelief, wanting to know when he was going to free Israel and restore the Kingdom. Jesus didn't mince words, he was honest that the Father had set the day and time, it wasn't for them to know. All they would know is that until that appointed time and day they were to remain on mission with the help of the Holy Spirit.

How easily we forget the simplicity of our assignment.

Jesus didn't leave them without instructions. He told them the Holy Spirit would come upon them and from there they were to be his witnesses, telling people everywhere of this saving knowledge of Jesus Christ in their local communities, neighboring cities, and countries, and all the way to the very edges of the earth. No pressure, right?

And as if that wasn't enough, Jesus was then taken up into a cloud until they could no longer see him, and I can imagine they looked at one another like, *Well, what's next?*

Have you ever felt that way? Okay, God, what's next? I've done everything you've asked of me; I've been following you for a while now, what's next? I have, and it is the most terrifying space to occupy and at the same time full of endless possibilities to run with Jesus.

I imagine those in the Upper Room felt the same way after their encounter with the Holy Spirit. Where could they possibly go from *this*? Literal tongues of fire sat on their heads; it couldn't get any crazier than that.

Or could it?

What if it was just the beginning?

As we read throughout the book of Acts, we find that the disciples and those who joined their mission would do exactly what they were instructed to do, moving from prayer meeting to prayer meeting, and finding themselves in both places of revival and places of resistance. Only through the power of the Holy Spirit would they remain on mission once the Church was born as the Lord added to their numbers daily through their obedience.

Mission: Jerusalem

The more I mature in Christ, the more ministry opportunities I find right in my own front yard: comforting a neighbor whose spouse has been sick, dog sitting, watering flowers, pulling in trash cans after dark, closing a garage door of my elderly neighbor who always forgets to close it before bed.

The Great Commission to go and make disciples sometimes means going front porch to front porch. Our Jerusalem might consist of a mom who craves a solo trip to Target while you hold her sleeping infant. Sometimes it's going city street to city street, serving in a shelter or cleaning up a school yard. Sometimes it's loading up a car with a few friends or our family and serving widows or taking books to an inner-city school and reading with kids after class.

Our ministry begins with loving our family, our neighbor, the grocery store clerk, the DoorDash guy, a parent at school, the congregant who always complains. When we're faithful in the small things, in the hidden places, we can be trusted with more. And God's people next door are just as important as God's people across the world.

We love them.

We serve them.

We make disciples *here and there*.

> God's people next door are just as important as God's people across the world.

Our mission at times will lead us to revival, and at other times it will meet us with great resistance.

It won't always be glamorous. There won't always be an adventure. You won't always get a photo op. But I can guarantee people will always meet Jesus through your authentic and genuine love for them.

Recently, a local church sent their student group to a nearby college campus with a table set up with free hot dogs and soda. Their sign simply read, "Ask a Christian a question and get a free hot dog!" The questions ranged from simple to complex, but their outreach met the students where they were in life—inquisitive, curious, intellectual—and opened up the door for the Gospel of Jesus Christ to be preached.

This is just one example of how we can reach our community. What are some other good ways to reach our Jerusalem?

- Team up with your neighborhood to pack backpacks for children who can't afford school supplies.
- Organize a Trunk-or-Treat in the church parking lot to get to know those who live near the church.
- Leave teachers gift baskets in their rooms or a meal in the teachers' lounge the first or last day of school and tell them thank you.
- Take bereavement baskets to hospitals for parents who have lost babies or who are in extended NICU.
- Memorize the name of your favorite baristas and thank them by name.
- Find out the favorite stores or food of your mechanic, nail tech, hair stylist, or mailman, and grab them a gift card just because.
- Drop cards into your neighbors' mailboxes and leave them words of encouragement.

Ministry is right where we are—all the time.

Mission: Judea and Samaria

If our Jerusalem is our neighborhood, those in our immediate proximity, then our Judea and Samaria extend just beyond our city limits to our state and country. Many of us are serving people beyond our backyards every single day, doing holy work outside the safety of an actual sanctuary as we take the Church into a lost world. We may never know the impact we've had until we get to heaven.

I unexpectedly met one of these servants in the summer of 2022. I was in a freak accident in my backyard while playing with my dog and a few other dogs from our neighborhood. I wish I could tell you I was doing something athletic, but I was just standing there and didn't get out of their way fast enough. They ran full speed in my direction and violently knocked me to the ground, where I hit my head on a rock.

I woke up in the hospital with a severe traumatic brain injury. The on-call doctor made it clear that I had been spared within a half inch of my life, as I hit the rock dangerously close to the side of my temple. The next few days were scary as I was told in no uncertain terms to lie in darkness without screens or sound to allow my brain to heal. I was plagued with severe vertigo, and I had temporary memory loss of the day.

The church where I served on staff was full of medical professionals who were at the top of their game—world-renowned surgeons, cancer specialists, you name it, we had them—and within a few hours of my accident, my phone was lighting up with doctors asking how they could help. One of the best brain surgeons in our state sent me a text that said, "Be in my office at 9 am sharp tomorrow morning." I knew he was booked out months in advance for new patients.

The next morning my husband drove me to the surgeon's office where the waiting room was bursting at the seams. Within ten minutes we were called to meet with him, and he spent nearly an hour with us. He reviewed my scans and then told me not only how I was going to heal physically, but what I needed to do to heal spiritually as my travel calendar was exploding due to my first book being close to launch. And for the next several months he was there, catching me in the church hallway to check my progress and to provide off-the-clock medical advice when a new symptom would arise.

That doctor pastored me as part of his Judea, and I'll never forget his ministry.

I love Ephesians chapter 4 where Paul commissions the church:

> In light of all of this, here's what I want you to do. While I'm locked up here, a prisoner for the Master, I want you to get out there and walk—better yet, run!—on the road God called you to travel. I don't want any of you sitting around on your hands. I don't want anyone strolling off, down some path that goes nowhere. And mark that you do this with humility and discipline—not in fits and starts, but steadily, pouring yourselves out for each other in acts of love, alert at noticing differences and quick at mending fences. (vv. 1–3 MSG)

Your mission likely looks different, but you carry the same Gospel. You minister in classrooms and boardrooms as you serve the least of these and support the most of these, loving those who have nothing or guiding those who have everything. Your sermons flow through lesson plans and medical reports, your prayers are whispered over a scared patient or frustrated coworker, and your worship flows from your car in rush hour. Ministry is wherever you are and wherever you go because you know the One who breaks chains and sets captives free, and you don't need the title of pastor to proclaim his name.

Don't let anyone tell you staying home with your babies, serving coffee in your community, bagging groceries, coaching, or creating isn't ministry. He has given you a field and workers and he trusts you with the harvest. Thank you for being the hands and feet of Jesus in unexpected places, for being on mission and commission where people are most vulnerable. You are the best of us as you go undercover and undetected as an ambassador of Christ.

> You pastor Monday to Friday in a world suspicious of Sunday. We need your ministry.

What a gift you are to the Church. You pastor Monday to Friday in a world suspicious of Sunday. We need your ministry.

Mission: Ends of the Earth

From a young age, I knew the Church was global. I watched my dad go to Russia and China, and he would come back with beautiful stories of salvation and miracles. I realized the Church wasn't confined to the US borders, and I wanted to meet other believers and those seeking who didn't look and sound like me.

My first mission trip out of the United States was to Mexico my senior year in high school. That trip would be the first of many to take me beyond the comfort of the American Church. When I went to places such as Haiti, I learned what true persecution looked like for my brothers and sisters in Christ and I witnessed raw faith for simple things I took for granted: food on my table, health care, schooling. Each time, I came back to my home country with a new perspective for ministry and it wasn't long before I found out the ends of the earth were also in my own backyard.

One of the best things my parents did was send me out of my country to see what God was doing around the world, as it not only educated me but shifted my vantage point from a national mind-set to a Kingdom mindset. I saw how my brothers and sisters in Christ from other parts of the world devoured the Scriptures like a five-course meal. I watched them secretly baptize one another in bathtubs filled with dirty water, emerging with an inexplicable joy, hands raised and tears streaming down their face. It would be easy to go on a mission trip and assume we are the ones blessing those we serve, when in reality, we are the ones being blessed by those we serve who don't look, sound, live, or worship the way we do.

The phrase "to the ends of the earth" appears forty-six times in the Scriptures, and though we tend to think it means leaving our country or homeland, it carries so much more meaning. God wants every single person in the entire world to know the Gospel. It could mean leaving your homeland ... it could mean crossing your street ... it could mean crossing the aisle, just go.

Because, Church, the ends of the earth or the nations could very well be your next-door neighbor.

By having an "ends of the earth" mindset in ministry, I am keeping Jesus on the throne. I take my identity as a child of God who is called to be the hands and feet of Jesus to everyone I meet, and I take the message of a risen Savior wherever I go. I remain on mission preaching Jesus, not stuck in a view of my personal experiences with Christianity, but with a biblical worldview.

How do we keep an "ends of the earth" mindset? We surround ourselves with as many opportunities as possible to have hard and holy conversations with those who don't look like us, sound like us, vote like us, or even believe like us. We wrestle with our faith, we wander unapologetically in looking for answers to big questions, and we sit across tables seeking to understand the views and experiences of others without demanding to first be heard.

As the Church, it will take every single one of us believing we have been called to shepherd those we live among and serve, willing to sit in the tension of not having the answers but daily pointing people to the One who does. It will mean being wrong, getting it wrong, and confessing when we've done things wrong and hurt others.

Only through truly loving and meeting people where they are can we develop the relational equity to go deeper into conversations of faith and salvation. As the old saying goes, people don't care how much we know until they know how much we care.

The Evangelistic Pastor versus the Local Church Pastor

After college I attended different churches and denominations, which challenged me in my faith and relationship with Jesus. I went to my first megachurch and served as an intern while teaching full time, and my eyes were opened to a whole new world of church culture. I became acquainted with the role of evangelical pastors who weren't convicted to stay in their local body and often brought in guest speakers or associate pastors to hold down the pulpit while they traveled, wrote books, and shared their wisdom with other congregations. There isn't anything wrong with that approach to ministry; in fact, there are pastors who do this very well, though I couldn't help but notice this was harder on the church staff and congregation than many realized.

The local pastor has a pulse on his staff and high-level volunteers. They are more readily available for funerals, weddings, staff meetings, and community events and they are oftentimes more approachable. Just as sheep learn to trust the shepherd leading them, the shepherd also learns the voice of the flock the more time they spend in the field alongside them.

When a church is being led by a well-intended pastor trying to live in the tension of both evangelist and local church pastor, the foundation can feel shaky, even if it is quite stable. Congregants and staff alike are looking for a leader who will be consistent and available, and holes in the foundation can easily allow the enemy access to the sheep. For many of us in leadership, we have felt this pull ourselves. We know we have a ministry inside of us, we know we are called to love the people of God, but it can be confusing when we begin to feel the discomfort of "going" beyond our local church walls.

For twenty years I served in the local church as a worship pastor and women's pastor. Most of my staff was tenured between three and five years while I was working two jobs—as a gym teacher and worship leader—in addition to raising two little girls. I was also feeling a pull toward leading worship and songwriting that could possibly take me into multiple churches out of state, and I had to be honest with those hiring me that I had a passion to minister and serve beyond one local church.

As Raised to Stay grew as a community and ministry, the writing was on the wall that my time on full-time staff in the local church might be coming to an end. It wasn't fair to the church and leadership for me to collect a paycheck when my heart and passion were shifting to a more evangelistic ministry mindset.

When we feel the call to "go," to leave a church and do ministry elsewhere, we should know that people can leave a church and nothing be wrong with said church. I recently had my own "going," and I was amazed at how quickly people assumed something was wrong. Was everything right? Of course not. There was some tension and misunderstanding and the enemy was looking to cause chaos and confusion, but my need to be obedient by faith with fear and trembling was stronger than the opinions of those I would be leaving behind. I knew it would be a hard season of hugging necks goodbye while reaching for new hellos.

> **We should know that people can leave a church and nothing be wrong with said church.**

Even in the imperfection of the church and the leaders I served alongside, I would have stayed on staff and in position, but I knew God wasn't asking me to leave, he was telling me to GO. In a perfect world I would have chosen to hold on to the good and contend for healthy culture as best I could, but if I couldn't do that, I would try my hardest to go in peace and be a blessing to those whom I had served beside for several years.

It seems no matter how purehearted we are in our going, people still want the inside scoop, the "real reason." We want to fan the flames of gossip rather than sit in the holy smoke of obedience that is costly and possibly even contagious.

Gossip divides. Obedience multiplies.

What if we're going because everything is right? What if everything is just as God is directing? What if even in the clunky reality that is human transition, there is honor, goodness, and blessing?

In Acts 13, we find Paul and Barnabas preaching the Gospel of Jesus Christ to the Gentiles, and Luke writes, "When the Gentiles heard this, they were very glad and thanked the Lord for his message; and all who were chosen for eternal life became believers. So the Lord's message spread throughout that region" (vv. 48–49).

But at the same time, we read in verse 50, "Then the Jews stirred up the influential religious women and the leaders of the city, and they incited a mob against Paul and Barnabas and ran them out of town."

And because going is complicated, Luke tells us, "So they shook the dust from their feet as a sign of rejection and went to the town of Iconium. And the believers were filled with joy and with the Holy Spirit" (vv. 51–52).

Paul and Barnabas's ministry was accepted by some and rejected by others, but it didn't mean their ministry was in vain. It was simply time to move on and they didn't even want to bring the dirt on their shoes with them to their next assignment.

If you're looking for a strategic blueprint in how to go, take note of this foundational principle: do not take old dirt into new seasons.

Hear me, brothers and sisters in the faith: when people decide to go, let them go. Don't provoke them, add to their story, diminish their choice, worry what is wrong, or make up false tales or endings. Going is part of this great race, and only the runners in tune with the voice of their coach know which lane to get in and how fast to run. Eyes up, legs ready, hearts bursting, lungs burning. They need cheers, not jeers.

We need to let others go with innocence and belief in their next seasons. We need to help unload their burdens of transition without piling on the weight of our offense. Nobody is so naive to believe their exit doesn't involve a few wounds, but they serve as blessings that reveal it is time to go and provide lessons for the season ahead. Allow people to choose to exit as victors, not victims.

We need to celebrate what they have done, mourn they will no longer be part of our big moments in life, and send them off with prayer and prophetic words, not doom and gloom. Watch how they go with grace, even if we want them to stomp out in fury. We can leave well; we can write the new narrative.

Our goals aren't longevity in a building or position, but obedience to Jesus and the Great Commission, faithfulness to a call. Grace for a new journey and gratitude for where we've been, good and bad. We want to run a new race free from anything God hasn't placed on our shoulders, unbothered, unhindered. We want the wind of the Holy Spirit at our back, not loaded down with the baggage of regret.

We need phone calls from friends looking forward with us, not looking back. We need prayers for where we're going, not reopening old wounds. And when we do this for each other, when we build together for a Kingdom purpose rather than tearing down, we will find unity together even while we're physically apart.

Transition is coming for many of us in the days ahead as we're being sent out to the far ends of the earth.

Let go with grace.

Speak life over where you've been with both honor and honesty.

Look forward with prophetic hope.

The future of a healed and healthy Church lies in our obedience to God and going out on his mission to bring as many people with us into his Kingdom, not our own.

Stay the course. God is sending the people and revival isn't far behind.

Reflection Prayer

"Dear God, I commit to staying on mission in both revival and resistance as I take the message of Jesus Christ to my neighbors, city, state, country, and to the ends of the earth. Break my heart and the heart of your Church for the things that break your heart. Give us a desire to see the lost found, the sick healed, and the bound set free. Put us back on mission, eyes set on you. Where you lead, I will follow."

Chapter 7

A HOUSE BUILT ON COMMUNITY

The Called and Courageous

"All the believers devoted themselves to the apostles' teaching, and to fellowship, and to sharing in meals (including the Lord's Supper), and to prayer. A deep sense of awe came over them all, and the apostles performed many miraculous signs and wonders."

Acts 2:42–43

When I was in elementary school my dad took a pastorate of a small United Church of Christ congregation in town. The church was built in the early 1800s and, at one time, had served as both a schoolhouse and a church, complete with a bell that rang out old hymns each hour. I remember spending hot summer days there as my dad studied for Sunday sermons. In that old one-room school-house church I stood behind the wooden pulpit preaching my first messages to my sister, who dramatically waved herself with a paper fan left behind in the pew and gave me a few courteous amens.

Lucille, our organist, had been around so long I assumed she came with the church. She didn't like it when the kids played her organ, but she made an exception for me, mostly because I was taking piano lessons and showed interest in her craft. She wore polyester skirts and nude pantyhose with special orthopedic shoes, her white hair twisted up into a messy bun and glasses perched at the end of her nose. Her feet didn't move quite as fast as they had in years before, so she would call me over to crawl under her bench and, using my hands, I would play the bass notes with fervor as she called out, "C!" "D!" "G!"

That's how I learned to play church piano, under the worn-out feet of a saint.

Lucille was a widow who lived in a small home nearby, and my dad often took my sister and me with him to visit her. He would take Communion and we knew if we behaved, she would let us pick out a cookie from her infamous blue cookie tin. (Some weeks it housed hard wrapped cinnamon candies.) There were a few times we tried to sneak something, and upon opening the precious lid as quietly as possible, we were devastated to find sewing materials inside. We would look up to see a sly smile on her face and we knew we'd been caught.

We loved these visits not only with Lucille but any time we got the chance to go with my parents to see church people. There was something special about being in their homes, even if we were too young to truly understand the purpose behind the house calls. Sometimes, it was to plan a wedding or a funeral. Other times, it was simply to check in on someone who hadn't been to church in a while. There were happy stops and others that made my mom cry once we were back in the car heading home. Sometimes, we went to say goodbye.

These visits were rarely convenient. I missed school events and the occasional birthday party or sleepover because we did ministry as a family. Once I became a teenager, I often felt impatient and annoyed. I was no longer able to be bribed with cookies and it was easy to have a bad attitude as we loaded into the car for another trip to visit a congregant in a neighboring town.

Yet it never failed; I left every visit encouraged by our time together and even more in love with the family of God.

Conveniently Inconvenienced

In Acts chapter 16, Luke introduces us to a businesswoman named Lydia who believed in God but hadn't yet been introduced to the Gospel of Jesus Christ. He describes her as a woman who sold purple cloth, and she is recorded as the first convert to the Christian faith in the Roman city of Philippi. God had told Paul to go to Macedonia near Philippi, and it "just so happened" Lydia and her entire family were there that same day where they heard the Good News of Jesus, believed, received, and were the first to be baptized by Paul.

Luke writes:

> On the Sabbath we went a little way outside the city to a riverbank, where we thought people would be meeting for prayer, and we sat down to speak with some women who had gathered there.

> One of them was Lydia from Thyatira, a merchant
> of expensive purple cloth, who worshiped God. As
> she listened to us, the Lord opened her heart, and
> she accepted what Paul was saying. She and her
> household were baptized, and she asked us to be
> her guests. "If you agree that I am a true believer
> in the Lord," she said, "come and stay at my home."
> And she urged us until we agreed. (Acts 16:13–15)

Lydia invites them to stay at her home and this everyday typical prayer meeting goes from being a transactional ministry opportunity to a relationship as she opens the doors to her home and invites these men to stay with her family in a beautiful display of hospitality.

How exciting is this? After all, isn't this the Great Commission to go and make disciples that we discussed in the previous chapter? This is exactly what Jesus commanded the disciples to do just prior to his ascension, and they are doing it! Luke and his entourage must have been on a spiritual high much like we are after a week on a mission trip leading people to Christ or a baptism service watching others come out of the water to new life. What a rush!

I like to imagine the conversation between the men as they left her home, reliving the past twenty-four hours. Were they in awe of the power and timing of God? After all, it wasn't on their itinerary. Were they high-fiving and hugging like we might do as we bring a fellow brother or sister up out of the water on baptism Sundays? The men were celebrating an entire family coming to know the saving grace of Jesus Christ when suddenly their story takes a turn.

"One day as we were going down to the place of prayer, we met a slave girl who had a spirit that enabled her to tell the future. She earned a lot of money for her masters by telling fortunes" (Acts 16:16).

Have you ever noticed that Satan rarely interrupts us on the way to a sporting event, girls' night out, or work? Yet the moment we're trying to get to church, Bible study, or night of prayer and worship, everything that could go wrong does go wrong?

Going on a mission trip? Expect a delayed flight.

Headed to the hospital to visit a congregant? Expect traffic.

Traveling to preach in a different state? Sick kid at home.

Planning a retreat for your team? Other sick kids at home.

He hates when the people of God make an intentional choice to be together in our Lord's presence, and he hated these men who were going city to city preaching the Gospel of salvation and freedom.

The enemy of our souls will do whatever he can to stop us from being together as the Church because he knows that where there is unity it commands the Lord's blessing!

"Behold, how good and how pleasant it is for brethren to dwell together in unity! ... It is like the dew of Hermon, descending upon the mountains of Zion; for there the LORD commanded the blessing—life forevermore" (Ps. 133:1, 3 NKJV).

> **Where there is unity it commands the Lord's blessing!**

Every time we try to do something good for God with the people of God, it always feels like we're interrupted. These men and their mission were no exceptions.

Luke, along with Paul and Silas, were leaving a powerful time of ministry with Lydia and her family, and I'm sure they couldn't wait to share the story with those attending their next scheduled prayer meeting. It was on their way to pray that Luke tells us they were interrupted by a young girl in bondage. She wasn't just a slave to her masters who used her to tell the future of others, she was a slave to the demon inside of her that enabled her to tell the future.

Luke writes, "She followed Paul and the rest of us, shouting, 'These men are servants of the Most High God, and they have come to tell you how to be saved'" (Acts 16:17).

Now it's personal.

She's giving away their identity in a place they didn't belong, nor were they wanted as Jews. This evil spirit bearing witness to the truth of who God is, echoing orthodox theology, with poor timing.

I try to imagine my response if I were walking the streets of a city in a different country where it was illegal to be a Christ follower and having someone follow me around screaming, "This is Natalie! She's a servant of Jesus Christ and she's here to tell you how to be saved!"

I have been in dangerous countries where I was obviously a for-eigner in an unknown land. It's been vital to our mission and safety to quietly preach the Gospel to those like Lydia and her family who have invited us in. If we were to be caught in the wrong place at the wrong time, it could mean fines, imprisonment, or worse, and that is exactly what happened in this scene.

As Jews, Paul and Silas were already walking around with giant targets on their backs.

Nobody would have blamed Paul if he had just ignored this young girl who had become a loud distraction and kept walking toward the prayer meeting. In fact, that would have been the safest option, yet Luke tells us that "this went on day after day until **Paul got so exasperated** that he turned and said to the demon within her, *'I command you in the name of Jesus Christ to come out of her'*" (Acts 16:18).

The word "exasperated" means that Paul was *grieved* for this little girl who was in captivity physically and spiritually. Grieved so much that he put his own safety and well-being at risk and confronted the very devil inside of her.

Upon reading this, I had to stop and ask myself: As a Christian in community with other believers, and as a neighbor and friend, when is the last time I have been grieved by watching those I love being held in bondage by the enemy? Grieved by sin? Grieved for those in oppression? When was the last time I let the Holy Spirit break my heart for those lost and enslaved to a master out to kill, steal, and destroy?

When was the last time I didn't worry about my reputation and revealed my Kingdom position by praying for someone in public, sharing the Good News of Jesus Christ or defending another brother or sister who was under attack?

I love that in this moment that could have brought chaos and confusion, Paul didn't have to Google "how to cast out a demon." Paul knew the authority he had in the name of Jesus Christ to speak one Name the devil couldn't stand against.

Paul was ready not only for the mission before him, but an inevitable prison that awaited him.

The scripture says, in that very moment, "instantly it [the demon] left her" (Acts 16:18).

Her masters became furious with Paul because they had lost their hope of more wealth. So they grabbed Paul and Silas and dragged them before the authorities in the marketplace, saying, "The whole city is in an uproar because of these JEWS! ... They are teaching customs that are illegal for us Romans to practice" (vv. 20–21).

Because Paul and Silas were Jews, they were immediately taken, beaten, and thrown into jail with a guard to keep watch over them.

Around midnight, they began singing hymns to God. Not sad songs of lament for being locked in a prison (even though that would have been appropriate and biblical in their position), but songs of praise as the other prisoners listened.

The Scriptures tell us that suddenly a massive earthquake shook the prison, and the chains of every prisoner fell off. But rather than trapping everyone under rubble, it set them free. God was shaking the very foundation of world powers, systems, and evil agendas.

He is still doing this today.

The jailer woke to see the prison doors wide open, and he assumed the inmates had escaped, so he drew his sword to kill himself. Luke writes in verse 28, "But Paul shouted to him, 'Stop! Don't kill yourself! We are all here!'"

They didn't leave.

Let's go back to the first part of Acts with the OG Stayers in the Upper Room who committed they were in this to the very end, come revival or resistance. Those in that room, and those who would join them now filled with the Holy Spirit, committed to their mission of preaching the Gospel of Jesus Christ.

Paul and Silas remained in position despite potential death and God showed up in that prison cell to prove himself to those in bondage as well as the prison guard. It wasn't the community they had expected to find on their way to the prayer meetings. It wasn't the crusade they had planned. It wasn't Instagram-worthy with big names and bands. It was an inconvenient interruption that turned to revival.

Many of us are leaving uncomfortable situations or the communities we didn't choose to save ourselves, and we are missing out on the miracle. Though we cannot stay where we aren't physically safe at the hands of abusers or narcissistic leaders, hard seasons and discomfort are often invitations to a miraculous display of God's power to us or those in spiritual chains around us.

> **Many of us are leaving uncomfortable situations or the communities we didn't choose to save ourselves, and we are missing out on the miracle.**

Paul and Silas demonstrated to the jailer—and even now to us as believers—that being disciples of Christ does not mean we try to escape difficult places, but we remain in position to be a safe place for the oppressed, bound, and hopeless.

When the people of God remained in position, they saw God reveal his true power.

- Shadrach, Meshach, and Abednego, after being thrown into the blazing furnace, were delivered from the flames by God (Dan. 3:16–28).

- Daniel, when sentenced to the lions' den, remained in position to see God close the mouths of those meant to devour him (Dan. 6:10–22).

- Noah, who built the ark even when everyone said he was crazy, was obedient to God's command and rode out the flood with his family unharmed (Gen. 7).

- Moses, who obeyed God's instructions to lead his people out of Egypt, remained in position to see God reveal his power by parting the Red Sea, bringing the Israelites to the other side to safety (Ex. 14:21–22).

- Esther, who went before the king with prophetic timing, trusted God to save her people from wicked Haman's plot to have them all destroyed, only to see Haman hung on the gallows he himself had made (Est. 5:1–8; 7:7–10 NKJV).

- Jesus suffered on the cross, who for the joy set before him remained in position knowing the resurrection was coming to reveal his true power (Heb. 12:1–2).

Sometimes, the smallest inconvenience that threatens to ruin our day will end up saving the day—or life—of another. Stay in position.

The Reward in the Ruins

It was Paul and Silas' obedience to stay where they were in the discomfort of rubble and uncertainty that compelled the jailer to ask, "What must I do to be saved?"

This is the question I want people asking me every single day as I obediently show up in places that might give away my identity as a Christ follower.

Jesus was very clear in what our mission would be as we went about our days. In Matthew 10:5–8 we read, "Jesus sent out the twelve apostles with these instructions: 'Don't go to the Gentiles or the Samaritans, but only to the people of Israel—God's lost sheep. Go and announce to them that the Kingdom of Heaven is near. Heal the sick, raise the dead, cure those with leprosy, and cast out demons. Give as freely as you have received!'"

Being in community means being conveniently inconvenienced so God can work in us and through us to make his glory known! It means we can be spiritually called and simultaneously confused in the flesh. God will still use our "yes" for his glory and make it all make sense later on. Through the power of the Holy Spirit, we have been appointed to:

> *Go and make disciples.*
> *Announce the Kingdom is coming.*
> *Heal the sick.*
> *Raise the dead.*
> *Cast out demons.*
> *Give freely.*

You may not feel qualified, educated, experienced, or prepared, but as people of God we have immediate access to the power of God that will cast out demons and set people free.

Have you stopped operating in your anointing because you got your feelings hurt (you felt ignored or unwanted) or weren't celebrated, and rather than press into the power of Christ you took your toys and went home?

God is looking for men and women who will sit in the midnight hour and hold the hand of a fellow brother or sister. To sing with them through the night until the foundations of addiction, lost identity, fear, depression, worry, and anxiety are shaken down, and who will remain to sit in the rubble and do what Paul and Silas did with their jailer and his family.

Paul and Silas gave a beautiful picture of the Church community from a prison cell:

- They delivered the true Gospel, the Word of the Lord.
- They stayed and served, knowing it could cost them their lives.
- They baptized in the name of the Father, the Son, and the Holy Spirit.
- They shared a meal.

I love how this entire story comes full circle. When you keep reading, and stay in God's story, like with Lydia and her family, you see the jailer and his household encounter the one true living God.

Paul and Silas eventually moved on, but in their willingness to be radically interrupted, the message and power of Jesus Christ continued to spread through the houses of Lydia and the jailer—even after they were long gone.

You and I carry the power of Jesus Christ in us, and he will use us, just like he used Paul and Silas and so many others to make his name and glory known.

"The Spirit of the LORD is upon me, for he has anointed me to bring Good News to the poor. He has sent me to proclaim that captives will be released, that the blind will see, that the oppressed will be set free, and that the time of the LORD's favor has come" (Luke 4:18–19).

Community Confessional

Even today I'm not much different than teenage Natalie who didn't want to miss a high school football game for ministry visits. I like my Friday nights watching Netflix and quiet mornings writing at Starbucks. There are some Sunday mornings I would rather stay in bed, but once I'm in the church building and greeted with hugs and sweet encouragement from the family of God, I am always so glad I decided to show up. So often we think our church needs us when, in reality, we need our churches. Yes, even you.

Community is a foundational piece to the Church that includes the good *and* the bad, the dawn *and* the midnight hour, the peaceful ocean *and* the raging seas, life *and* death. Without authentic community, we're just religious robots coming in and checking boxes and then alone the rest of the week without friendship, encouragement, and discipleship.

This world is lonely, desperate to be part of something and have a cause, what we term a purpose. You and I are no different; just because we're Christians doesn't mean we don't need help or friendship. And if we don't need anyone now, one day we will when we get the scary test result, lose a spouse or a child, move to a new city, or need a shoulder to cry on. Yes, we have Jesus, but God created his children to be part of his family, and we can't do that running from spiritual high to spiritual high. We find true families in spiritual prisons singing through the night believing and waiting for a breakthrough.

Whomever we, as the Church, fail to care for, the world will receive with open arms.

> Whomever we, as the Church, fail to care for, the world will receive with open arms.

There are counterfeit communities all around us who will promise solidarity but leave us in solitude. When the deconstruction movement began to sweep through social media platforms, there were hundreds of accounts dedicated to walking with people through the process. Though some offered healthy dialogue and conversation, many lacked a solid foundation to provide any real help to those looking for answers. They promised healing only to lick wounds with their saltiness. They offered sweet revenge, but it was a mere cup of bitterness.

One example of this counterfeit community came from a group of individuals who were raised in the Church, hurt by the Church, and spent their days doing their best to destroy the Church. I would read their posts and feel my cheeks flush with anger as they mocked God and Christians and used profanity and vulgar memes to gain followers. They promised those joining their many different platforms a place to feel seen, heard, and validated in their pain but offered no solution of healing.

Their entire community depended on people remaining bitter to grow.

I was amazed at how quickly this particular account gained popularity seemingly overnight, but just as quickly as it rose, it fell with an anticlimactic thud not long after. Citing irreconcilable differences, the account's leaders all went their separate ways, leaving their followers in the dust. Division and bitterness make horrible foundations when trying to build something that will last.

The Church has a beautiful opportunity to provide a safe and healthy community for those asking the big questions, yet we don't always know how to start the conversations, in fear we won't have answers. I have been inspired by many churches who have opened their doors to programs such as Celebrate Recovery and Alpha, which offer weekly opportunities for those with hurts, habits, and hang-ups to find refuge on holy ground.

Counterfeit communities will feed off our pain for their gain.

Christlike communities will lead us to the Healer, Jesus Christ.

Once people find their way into our doors, our community can be Christ through first-impression teams, care pastors, small group opportunities, ministries for every stage of life, and connection points beyond Sunday-morning services.

Church, we must be willing to contend for Christlike community. That word *contend* means "to agonize." It is the spirit of true agony that possesses one who is contending. "Agony of spirit and love for the Gospel should be in the *heart of every believer*. Contending means to fight while standing on the very thing being assaulted. It means to stand *against* all who undermine it."[6]

Are we willing to contend for community in our churches while living in a world that is assaulting God's Church and encouraging people to walk away from not only the Church family but also their Heavenly Father? Are we willing to be disrupted on our way to our next thing in order to see spiritual orphans who are seeking a place to belong?

Community comes to the committed. Those willing to show up, serve, lead, and remain in position even when they don't feel worthy or prepared. Community comes to those who are honest in their struggles, bondage, and fears of being hurt again, but who are desperate for freedom and friendship.

Are our churches a safe place for those struggling to find a Savior?

Are we, as leaders, willing to have our lives interrupted to see others encounter the power of God?

God is shaking the foundations of this world, preparing to return for a Church built on Christ, the true Cornerstone.

May he find his Church faithful and standing strong in the ruins.

Reflection Prayer

"God, I confess there are days your people wear me out and wear me down and I hide from community. I want friendship, but I fear I will be hurt again. I want to get back into a church but I'm afraid

I'll be disappointed, and I don't know if I have another disappointment in me. I long for an Upper Room community, show me how I can be part of building that with you in my church and even my neighborhood. Show me the Lydias looking for you and those living in bondage desperate for freedom. I am willing to be radically inconvenienced for the Kingdom."

Chapter 8

A HOUSE BUILT ON WORSHIP

Songs and Swords

"They worshiped together at the Temple each day, met in homes for the Lord's Supper, and shared their meals with great joy and generosity— all the while praising God and enjoying the goodwill of all the people."

Acts 2:46–47

As a preacher's kid, every time the doors were open—for church services, revivals, camp meetings, funerals, weddings, or Bible study—I was there front and center mostly because I knew it would include a potluck served by a saint with the spiritual gift of mac 'n' cheese. We ate all the time; there wasn't a restaurant who didn't recognize our caravan coming through their front doors or a home we weren't welcome. There were nights the conversation around the table went from casual small talk to prayer meetings.

Yes, being in church on Sunday mornings was powerful, but it was the day-to-day life together that bonded us as family. When we loved, we loved big, and when we fought, we fought hard, and when there was hurt, it was unlike any hurt we had ever experienced before.

Every time we gathered as the family of God, it was an act of worship: not limited to singing or musical instruments, but through living life together around tables and bonfires, hospital beds and living rooms.

One of the great lies we have believed is that worship starts and ends with the first and last notes of the Sunday-morning setlist, but music is one form of worship, not the definition of worship.

We have confined worship to an experience, when it's meant to be a lifestyle not lived alone.

Worship is a beautiful part of his blueprint, Church.

> **We have confined worship to an experience, when it's meant to be a lifestyle not lived alone.**

The Samaritan woman was one of the first to ask Jesus a question regarding worship, "So tell me, why is it that you Jews insist that Jerusalem is the only place of worship, while we Samaritans claim it is here at Mount Gerizim, where our ancestors worshiped?" (John 4:20).

Jesus responded with great intentionality:

> Believe me, dear woman, the time is coming when
> it will no longer matter whether you worship the

> Father on this mountain or in Jerusalem.... But
> the time is coming—indeed it's here now—when
> true worshipers will worship the Father in spirit
> and in truth. The Father is looking for those who
> will worship him that way. For God is Spirit, so
> those who worship him must worship in spirit and
> in truth. (John 4:21, 23–24)

Jesus didn't take offense but instead brings freedom in his answer, reminding us worship has never been about a location or a physical building. What matters in our worship is the posture of our hearts and minds and spirits as we live our lives for God in Christ.

I began this chapter with Luke describing how the first church "worshiped together at the Temple each day, met in homes for the Lord's Supper, and shared their meals with great joy and generosity—all the while praising God and enjoying the goodwill of all the people" (Acts 2:46–47).

In just these two verses alone, we see how the first church in Acts worshipped together in numerous ways. The following worship basics can be added to our blueprint for the modern-day church:

- corporate worship
- communal worship
- joyful worship
- generous worship
- unified worship

When the people of God gather, we can't help but worship.

When the people of God come together to worship the one true God, he meets with us and dwells among us.

A House of "SAY SO"

The psalmist writes, "Has the LORD redeemed you? Then speak out! Tell others he has redeemed you from your enemies" (Ps. 107:2). In other words, don't hold back telling others what our mighty God, our good Father, has done for you!

I love the church services that turn into the mic being passed from saint to saint as they share testimonies of what God has done in their lives.

Those prodigals they have been praying for the last several years? Sitting beside them. The cancer? Gone! The financial crisis? Provided for. The marriage? Restored. The addiction? Set free.

As some testify of deliverance, healing, peace, freedom, and salvation, the faith of those in the room is raised up and strengthened too. Weary heads are lifted, hopeless hearts begin to beat, downcast souls look up, and worried minds begin to clear ... we're reminded that our God can do anything and in these moments our faith increases at the sound of their "say so."

Once when I was ministering in Canada, a young mom came running down the aisle with her small son in her arms during the altar call. Now around three years old, this boy had been born with an illness that affected his ability to walk and his mom was desperate to see her child healed. We gathered all the pastors around them and began to pray for God to align every muscle, tendon, and bone to perfection so her baby could walk, run, and have full range of motion in his lower extremities.

That day nothing happened. This sweet mama carried her son out just as she had when they came down the aisle.

Three months later, I received a direct message in Instagram from an unknown account. The mom from Canada was sharing a video of her son with the simple caption, "Take up your bed and walk." It showed him at their local park running across a soccer field and climbing on the playground equipment.

I wept as I watched this clip over and over. Her "say so" strengthened my faith and the faith of many others. As the video made its way around social media—and to those who prayed in the room that day—we all came together believing God anew for his miraculous healing. While the video of her young son walking was truly remarkable, her intentionality to send me a message to share in the miracle and celebrate with her was equally as powerful and strengthened my faith. In that moment, her family felt like my family, and I was reminded we're never alone in our struggles or victories when we're part of the family of God.

Release your "say so"!

We also see this beautifully modeled in Scripture in the story of Rahab. Although her initial reputation was as a harlot, her legacy is woven beautifully into the family of God for protecting God's people when she hid two Israelite spies in her home. In Joshua chapter 2, Rahab told the spies how she had come to know of their God.

> Before the spies went to sleep that night, Rahab went up on the roof to talk with them. "I know the LORD has given you this land," she told them. "We are all afraid of you. Everyone in the land is living

in terror. For we have heard how the LORD made
a dry path for you through the Red Sea when you
left Egypt. And we know what you did to Sihon
and Og, the two Amorite kings east of the Jordan
River, whose people you completely destroyed. No
wonder our hearts have melted in fear! No one has
the courage to fight after hearing such things. For
the LORD your God is the supreme God of the
heavens above and the earth below. (vv. 8–11)

It made no sense that Rahab, who lived in the evil and corrupt
Jericho under God's wrath, would know the Israelites' God. Yet
somehow, the say so of the Israelites had made its way to her and
she had heard of God who had parted seas and destroyed enemies.
Their testimonies led her to the saving conclusion, "For the LORD
your God is the supreme God of the heavens above and the earth
below" (v. 11).

Their say so not only allowed the Israelites to come in and
conquer Jericho, but Rahab came to the knowledge of God and
exchanged her dead-end occupation for a legacy of protector of God's
people that landed her in the genealogy of Jesus Christ: "Salmon was
the father of Boaz (whose mother was Rahab)" (Matt. 1:5).

The impact of their say so was far more powerful than the pagan
culture around Rahab.

Do we believe that our say so carries more power than the
influence of the culture around us? What if our testimony of God's
goodness, strength, comfort, and provision in our lives was louder
than the voice of the current culture around us?

What if our say so brought others into a loving relationship with the saving knowledge of God the Father?

What is your say so? When is the last time you shared your story of how God brought you out, carried you through, held you up, and comforted your soul when you were down?

The world is waiting to hear.

My Worship Is a Weapon

In the last chapter we visited Paul and Silas as they turned their prison cell into a sanctuary. Many of us have been in similar spots, worshipping our way through the night by turning hospital rooms, offices, cars, and living rooms into sacred spaces as we've come face to face with death, fear, anxiety, and hopelessness.

Just as Jonah prayed, "In trouble, deep trouble, I prayed to GOD. He answered me. From the belly of the grave I cried, 'Help!' You heard my cry" (Jon. 2:2 MSG).

In this very dark night of the soul, we often find worship is our only weapon.

A couple of years after I had my youngest daughter, I found myself in a dark place. I had never struggled with anxiety, but that winter brought so much fear—of death, loss, sickness—that it began to affect me physically. After a few months of sleepless nights, restless days, migraines, dizziness, and feeling as if I were having a heart attack, I put my two little girls in the car and drove myself to the emergency room. I had convinced myself I was dying and my daughters would be left without a mother.

My husband was at work, so my in-laws drove over to pick up the girls while I went through a battery of tests to pinpoint the cause of these symptoms. After several hours, I found myself alone in the hospital room and caught a glimpse of my reflection in the mirror. I barely recognized myself: hair disheveled, pale, twenty-five extra pounds weighing heavy on me. It felt as if I were staring at a stranger.

A full-time worship leader at this time, every Sunday I was leading songs of healing and deliverance over the people of God while the room spun, my mind whirled, and my heart raced, certain I was on death's doorstep. I wanted desperately to believe the words were true, but it felt as if they were true for everyone else but me. This silent battle made me feel so isolated and alone, as if I were the only one struggling for air while others floated safe above the waters. I had spent so much time singing over others; where were those who would sing these same songs of assurance and deliverance over me?

You never know what people leading you each Sunday are silently struggling with deep in their own hearts.

I was discharged from the hospital with medication for migraines and vertigo and instructions to lose some weight, drink more water, and sleep eight hours a night. As a working mom of two, that advice felt impossible to achieve, but at least knowing my heart and brain were functional gave me peace for the next twenty-four hours.

I wish I could tell you after that day all my symptoms ceased and I was miraculously healed, but in the following weeks, things continued to escalate, silently, as I didn't want to worry my family.

Until one morning, while doing the dishes, I had enough.

My oldest was at school and my two-year-old was watching cartoons on the couch while I stood over the sink in PJ pants. The room was spinning, my head was throbbing, but I decided to go to war in worship. My kitchen became a sanctuary as I blasted the song "No Longer Slaves" through the room and fell to my knees sobbing uncontrollably.

I laid my hands on my whirling head, my eyes now spilling tears—offering my lungs, my heart, my stomach, my feet in worship—and stood up under an open heaven. I began to dance … to sing … to pour out my worship at the feet of Jesus though my head felt as if it might explode and my tears burst into flames as I believed *every word* in those lyrics:

> You split the sea
> So I could walk right through it
> My fears are drowned in perfect love
> You rescued me
> So I could stand and say
> I am a child of God.[7]

And then I did what might seem insane to some: I urgently started searching for Communion elements. I had never taken Communion like this before—outside of a church service or special holiday event, all alone in my pajamas using a juice box and Goldfish crackers—but I could sense in my spirit my Father inviting me to the Table.

I ran to the playroom, my youngest quietly occupied in the other room, and sat at the plastic table-and-chair set that was far too small for me. I looked at the empty chair across from me, but it wasn't empty. I was looking deep into the eyes of Jesus.

I had been doing motherhood, marriage, and ministry without him, trying to do it all on my own and I was flailing, failing miserably. Every week I was showing up for other people and leading them into the presence of God, but I had neglected my own heart and relationship with God in the process.

Brothers and sisters in Christ, we cannot sacrifice our own relationship with Jesus in an effort to strengthen others' relationships with Jesus.

We must serve from overflow, not leftovers.

The day my kitchen turned into a sanctuary changed me. The moment my worry turned to worship and warfare taught me how to fight on my knees, not in my head. God's invitation to join him at his table in the middle of a Wednesday morning reminded me that every moment of every day is a call into his presence; it's the only place we will find rest and rescue.

> **We must serve from overflow, not leftovers.**

I don't know where you are today, but I pray you'll hear an invitation from your Father to come and dine, to come and abide, so the storms of life won't consume you in your attempt to love and lead others. A life of worship commands dropping our dishes, microphones, spreadsheets, emails, and social media to grab a juice box and a few Goldfish crackers ... to sit across from Jesus wherever we are ... to be recentered on his gaze.

Lord, we set our eyes on you.

Sometimes Worship and Wailing Sound the Same

Not long ago, our precious border collie, Bear, was hit by a truck in our cul-de-sac and his leg was so badly damaged we were forced to amputate. It was only the second week at a brand-new school for my then eleven-year-old, and I knew it would be better for Selah to be in school while we had Bear at the vet hospital. That morning, rather than having her take the bus, we drove the back roads of Kentucky together in silence, her sitting in the front seat. Her little hands were perfectly clasped in her lap as she gazed out the window, her eyes full of tears threatening to fall at any moment.

I grabbed her hand and started thanking God for the gift that Bear was to our family and how God used him to bring us joy and protection and laughter. Right there in our little Toyota SUV, God met my daughter and me in a time of thanksgiving and lament, because God meets us in *both* expressions of worship. We don't have to gaslight ourselves into believing everything is always good all the time. Our children need to see us wrestling with God in situations that feel unfair and unkind. They need to hear us praying, weeping, rejoicing, and worshipping in freedom, not fearing what people will think.

> Our children need to see us wrestling with God in situations that feel unfair and unkind.

In Acts 16:25, we see Paul and Silas sitting in their prison cell and we're told, "Around midnight Paul and Silas were praying and singing hymns to God, and the other prisoners were listening."

I don't know about you, but I struggle with nighttime. During the day I am busy and my thoughts are on the many tasks in front of me, but as soon as my head hits the pillow, I'm a prisoner to regret, fear, and insecurity. As someone who has struggled with anxiety, the midnight hour can be filled with Googling mysterious symptoms ailing my body, rethinking old conversations and scenarios, and waking up to every creak in the house as I beg sleep to find me.

Paul and Silas were in their own literal midnight hour, but rather than worry and focus on their circumstances, they began to pray and worship, and it says in the Scriptures that the "other prisoners were listening" (v. 25).

What should we take away from this?

Those in bondage to this world are watching us as Christ followers to see how we will respond to the midnight hour.

The cancer diagnosis.

The divorce.

Our prodigal.

The loss of a child.

A season of unemployment.

Financial struggles.

Will we worry or will we worship?

There are sounds we can't un-hear. For me as a church kid, it was the wailing of saints in the pews begging God to bring home their prodigal. It was praying in living rooms for God to restore a marriage. It was the silent sobs of a mother in her birthing room asking for a miracle. It's a groan like no other. It's animalistic, primal, raw, a sound I could identify without looking up.

Because sometimes worship and wailing sound the same, but I learned they come from two different places. One from what God has already done and the other from a deep hope of what we long for him to do.

I remember the first time I distinguished the difference between someone worshipping from a place of gratitude and worshipping from a place of deep sorrow because it woke me up. Yes, joyful music is wonderful but true godly sorrow is transformational. And we need both in the House of God. Both have changed me.

From far away one might not be able to tell the worship from the wailing, but it reaches the throne of heaven equally. It's a sound I'll never forget. It's a sound that kept drawing me back into the House of God and into the homes of the saints and it's possible this sound led me into an early ministry of worship leadership. I got to be part of both the celebration and the transformation, in the lives of the congregation as well as my own.

Holy lament is a song few want to sing, but it's our worship penned in the dark night of the soul that writes a mournful melody in a minor key. We're singing over those who have suffered great loss, wrestling with anger, contending for peace, waiting for answers, grieving, weeping, suffering.

May we be a people who worship and wail, shouting his salvation and mourning with sweet brokenness his amazing grace.

When the Church Worships

When the Church worships, lives are changed, regardless of if we're singing an actual song or using our worship as a weapon against our enemy.

We don't worship because we got the outcome we wanted, the test results we prayed for, or the miracle we felt we were promised, but because God promises that when we worship and pray, he will be among us. Where the Spirit of the Lord is, there is freedom and unity.

In the book of Acts, Luke continues to describe what was happening in the early Church as the spirit of God fell among them and the Church was being added to daily:

> A deep sense of awe came over them all, and the apostles performed many miraculous signs and wonders. And all the believers met together in one place and shared everything they had. They sold their property and possessions and shared the money with those in need. They worshiped together at the Temple each day, met in homes for the Lord's Supper, and shared their meals with great joy and generosity—all the while praising God and enjoying the goodwill of all the people. And each day the Lord added to their fellowship those who were being saved. (2:43–49)

When our dog was hit by the truck and lost his leg, it was an invitation to holy lament for our family. But it also became an invitation to our church community to sit with us in the sorrow and rejoice with us in his healing. Notes of encouragement and cards came in, others sent meals, and my social media accounts were filled with messages from the Raised to Stay community who had walked through similar situations with their dogs. Our community didn't act like it was "just a dog," but as if he was part of our family. Many won't know how much it meant to us that we weren't alone in something that some would deem silly but that was so important to us.

As the Church we show up to worship together.

We open our homes and our tables with great generosity.

We bring what we have been given to share with others.

We take joy in the gathering of the saints.

We welcome others to the family of God.

Now that is a Church Jesus would be proud of.

Reflection Prayer

"Dear God, help me to be a worshipper in spirit and in truth. I want to worship you in every word I say and in everything I do, making your Name known in all seasons and in all circumstances. I don't want it to be confined to music or songs, but a lifestyle on my knees in surrender giving glory and honor to you and you alone. Teach us, your Church, how to worship again. Forgive me for making it about anything but you. I worship you, Jesus."

PART 3

REFRAMING

THE FLOORPLAN AND FRAMEWORK

"A house is built by wisdom and becomes strong through good sense. Through knowledge its rooms are filled with all sorts of precious riches and valuables."

Proverbs 24:3–4

Chapter 9

WE WILL BE A HOUSE OF FORGIVENESS

Repentance and Renaissance

"It may well be that we will have to repent in this generation. Not merely for the vitriolic words and the violent actions of the bad people, but for the appalling silence and indifference of the good people who sit around and say, 'Wait on time.'"[8]

Martin Luther King Jr.

When I was a little girl, I tended to stretch the truth. Call me creative, imaginative, colorful if you will, but I was a little liar. I had absolutely no reason to lie to anyone, but my needs for approval and to fit in, to contribute or feel important, often brought out big tales from my small mouth until one day I got caught.

I was in elementary school, it was Christmastime, and I told my sweet teacher a bold-faced lie. I told her we owned a popular Christmas movie on VHS, never expecting her to call my mom and ask for permission to borrow it for our class to watch the week before Christmas vacation. But not only did we not own the movie, we didn't even own a VHS player. Clearly, my mom was surprised by my teacher's call and confronted me over dinner that night.

At first, I denied any wrongdoing, but after several minutes I confessed to lying to my teacher. But it wasn't over. As a pastor's daughter in a very small town where we knew nearly everyone, my mom wasn't about to let me off the hook. She personally hauled my butt to school early the next morning so I could confess that I had lied to my teacher and ask for her forgiveness.

At first, I was sorry I got caught. I was embarrassed and annoyed at my mom for making such a big deal out of it and not covering for me. I was just a kid! After my mom left to go to work, I went to wash my tear-soaked face in the bathroom. As I stared into the mirror I felt relief, like a knot in the pit of my stomach had been untied and I was free. How heavy that little white lie had been on my little life in such a short amount of time.

I have carried that memory with me for nearly forty years because of what the Holy Spirit taught me that day:

I learned the importance of going to the person I offended *in person* and asking them to forgive me for how I hurt them. Though it was the hardest thing to do at seven years old—and even now as an adult—going straight to the source and seeking forgiveness brings such freedom and healing when the enemy wants to cause chaos and pain.

I learned about true repentance. The Bible teaches us that repentance is a change of heart and life when it comes to our sin. It is woefully turning from our sinful, wicked ways and moving toward God to be forgiven and set apart. We repent because we have sinned against God and we want to be forgiven. When we repent, we are acknowledging our need for God's forgiveness and grace. We are then made new. I didn't want to continue lying to those I loved, and as a child with an exaggerative imagination that would follow me into adulthood, I would have to work hard not to lie to make a story better or to fit in.

I also discovered the beauty of being forgiven. I left the bathroom and returned to my classroom, which was beginning to fill with classmates who were oblivious to what had transpired moments before. My teacher was waiting at the door in her Christmas jean jumper to give me my morning hug—just as she did every morning—as if nothing had happened. She didn't punish me the rest of the day; we never spoke of it. Her forgiveness and kindness made me never want to lie to her again.

Repentance Brings Change

Clearly, this experience changed me as a person. Would I still tell a lie from time to time? Of course, but it came with immediate conviction and a prayer asking God to forgive me. Becoming a Christian doesn't make us exempt from sin, but we are grieved when we do. I didn't want to lie, and the sweet correction of the Holy Spirit was right there to remind me that I was created to live and speak truthfully. True repentance doesn't just stir us up for a moment, it changes us.

> **Becoming a Christian doesn't make us exempt from sin, but we are grieved when we do.**

Can you imagine if those in the Upper Room were merely stirred up by the Holy Spirit and not actually changed? They would need the same power that fell among them in the days, weeks, months, and years ahead to remind them they were committed to finishing what had been started among them.

I love how Paul encourages Timothy by telling him, "This is why I remind you to fan into flames the spiritual gift God gave you when I laid my hands on you" (2 Tim. 1:6), meaning if you don't use it you'll lose it. Some translations say to "stir up the gifts," reminding us not to grow stagnant and let all the good stuff settle to the bottom of our hearts.

The gifts God gave Timothy were to be used and exercised so they would increase as he was obedient to do the work set before him. Paul knew his young protégé would need encouragement to stay on course and complete his mission: "For God has not given us a spirit of fear and timidity, but of power, love, and self-discipline" (v. 7). Paul knew from personal experience that fear was powerful enough to stop Timothy from fully operating in the gifts, primarily fear of man, as he traveled and preached the Gospel of Jesus Christ.

One of the most powerful forms of idolatry we let into our lives is fear of man. We spend countless hours worrying about what people think of us—precious time trying to prove ourselves for a pat on the back from another human who has no authority over our anointing or assignment. We have no control over their perception of us; our only responsibility and loyalty is to Christ, who has ordered our steps and given us his Word to carry. Nobody can stop what God has started in us, so pick up that mantle and run with confidence in what you've been given.

I have struggled with fear of man and acceptance most of my life. I've come face to face with rejection and indifference to the gifts God has given me. While I was waiting for nods of approval and words of affirmation from mere mortals, the Holy Spirit was waiting for me to stir up the gifts he had given me and use them unapologetically to help build his Kingdom.

Any time we allow the voice of man to be louder than the voice of God in our lives, we have irreverently elevated a mortal over the Living God. The Lord spoke similarly to Jeremiah, saying, "Don't say, 'I'm too young,' for you must go wherever I send you and say whatever I tell you. And don't be afraid of the people, for I will be with you and will protect you" (Jer. 1:7–8).

Not everyone will understand you. I know how hard it is to know you're loved but not always liked by those you admire. Just keep going; don't let their noise or loud silence discourage or distract you. Time is too short to let the voice of a few critics overpower the voice of your Creator. Listen for the Lord who is giving you daily instructions through his Word and Holy Spirit. God has not given you a spirit of fear. You won't win everyone over, but that is not your battle to be won. Be strong and courageous, eyes fixed on Jesus with a heart that trusts "the LORD is for me, so I will have no fear. What can mere people do to me?" (Ps. 118:6).

> **God has not given you a spirit of fear. You won't win everyone over, but that is not your battle to be won.**

When it comes to repentance, it's important to first look within and ask the Lord to search our hearts for anything sinful or deceitful. I often have to pray:

> "God, forgive me for exalting man's voice over your voice."
>
> "God, I repent for caring more about what people think than what you think."
>
> "God, please forgive me for not using the gifts you have given me or not being obedient to what you told me to do because I was afraid of what others would think."

It isn't easy to look inward first, but repentance is part of stirring up the gifts from God inside us that the enemy hopes we will let die out of fear, timidity, and insecurity. When we humble ourselves before the Lord and turn from our wicked ways, he promises to heal our land.

"Then if my people who are called by my name will humble themselves and pray and seek my face and turn from their wicked ways, I will hear from heaven and will forgive their sins and restore their land" (2 Chron. 7:14).

It starts with each of us. As we fall to our knees in godly sorrow for our sins and turn from our wicked ways to fix our eyes on Jesus, we will see a Church rise up out of the rubble with a strength no scheme of the enemy can stand against.

Hear us from heaven, oh God. Forgive us for every sin that has caused division among us and hurt your people. Come and heal our land; come and heal your Church.

When I think back to the little girl with the tear-soaked face in her elementary school bathroom, whose stomach was no longer knotted up in conviction but free to start a new day with new grace and mercy, I think of this passage from Hebrews 12:

> Therefore, since we are surrounded by such a huge crowd of witnesses to the life of faith, let us strip off every weight that slows us down, especially the sin that so easily trips us up. And let us run with endurance the race God has set before us. We do this by keeping our eyes on Jesus, the champion who initiates and perfects our faith. Because of the joy awaiting him, he endured the cross, disregarding its shame. Now he is seated in the place of honor beside God's throne. (vv. 1–2)

Today is a good day to lay down our sin, turn our sorry to sorrow, and trust that he will bring joy in the morning as we run toward the Saving One.

From Sorry to Sorrowful

Isn't God just like this to us, his children? Paul writes in Romans 2:4, "Don't you see how wonderfully kind, tolerant, and patient God is with you? Does this mean nothing to you? Can't you see that his kindness is intended to turn you from your sin?"

The *Message* version of this same scripture reads, "God is kind, but he's not soft. In kindness he takes us firmly by the hand and leads us into a radical life-change." God's kindness leads us to this same repentance I learned about at seven years old, welcoming us back with new mercies every morning. He doesn't hold grudges or harp on our latest sin. He isn't keeping score or putting us on lists that he checks twice. His Word tells us that he casts our sin as far as the east is from the west, and when we repent and turn from our ways, we are forgiven and set free from the weight of our sin and shame that Jesus carried for each of us to Calvary.

Feeling sorry about our sin is part of the process, but it's not the end. It's true sorrow that leads to repentance and convicts us to turn away from our sin, to change course, and to run toward Jesus. Paul described this: "Now I rejoice, not that you were made sorry, but that your sorrow led to repentance. For you were made sorry in a godly manner, that you might suffer loss from us in nothing" (2 Cor. 7:9 NKJV). Paul wasn't glad for the suffering or the situation that had brought the church of Corinth to this place of sorrow, but he was rejoicing that because of their sorrow they were being led toward the saving knowledge of Jesus Christ through salvation.

When was the last time you weren't just sorry for your sin, but truly sorrowful? The kind of sorrow that leads you to the feet of Jesus in true repentance that brings change of behavior (such as surrender of idols and addictions) and a shift in direction that will allow you to run your race freely?

Repentance Leads to Salvation

All homes require a skeletal structure, called the "frame," to give them support. While unseen, how it is formed is important because it provides shape and a framework for all the intricate outer design we appreciate. Newer homes utilize steel framing; however, older homes were often made from wooden beams, floor joists, wall studs, roof rafters, and other materials found in the locale.

The same applies when building a church. You need to work with the best materials when constructing the framework for your structure.

Repentance is talked about in Acts more than any other book in the Bible. Following the Holy Spirit's arrival and Peter's powerful sermon, Luke tells us, "Peter's words pierced their hearts, and they said to him and to the other apostles, 'Brothers, what should we do?' Peter replied, 'Each of you must repent of your sins and turn to God'" (Acts 2:37–38).

Peter was well qualified to preach this powerful sermon: he knew the Gospel of Jesus Christ firsthand, a brand-new revelation and conversation for them, as some of them had just witnessed a resurrected Jesus and ascending King. Peter personally understood the power of repentance, the true sacrifice Christ had made, and the promise of forgiveness for those who turn to God and away from their sin. Before moving forward to share the Gospel, it was vital the early Church be founded upon the repentant hearts of the people.

As today's Church sits in the rubble, repentance will be critical for the spiritual renaissance we are all desperate for—a radical renewal and revival.

Jumping ahead to Acts 3:17–19, after Peter publicly healed the lame man, he noticed a crowd had gathered and took the opportunity to preach the full Gospel of Jesus Christ. He said, "Friends, I realize that what you and your leaders did to Jesus was done in ignorance. But God was fulfilling what all the prophets had foretold about the Messiah—that he must suffer these things. Now repent of your sins and turn to God, so that your sins may be wiped away."

Peter took the time to acknowledge the elephant in the room; many had been ignorant to who Jesus was and still carried guilt for their part in his crucifixion. In regard to Jesus' true identity and mission, they had been led astray, misguided, perhaps manipulated and lied to by other religious leaders.

Many of us have also been misled by those we thought we could trust, innocently partnering with leaders and movements that in the end caused us to sin, hurt others, and be part of divisive situations that affected our church and those we love.

If you recall in chapter 4, I told the story of how my former supervisor used me to correct a fellow coworker and then went behind my back as if I were the problem. A couple of years after the incident, I ran into that coworker, who was no longer employed with me at the church. On a warm summer night we stood in the middle of a sidewalk, and I repented for my part in the situation: for not standing up to our boss, for not refusing to be part of her scheme, and for the hurt it had caused my friend. There were tears and hugs, and ultimately forgiveness and reconciliation.

We have the same assurance Peter gave God's people in Acts: though they were led astray, Jesus truly is the Son of God. If they would repent and turn from their sins toward God, their sins would be forgiven.

Those in the room that day went from sorry to sorrowful. To just be sorry means we regret we were caught, are embarrassed, and will try in our own flesh not to do it again. To be sorrowful means allowing God to break our hearts for the sins that have weighed us down and choosing to turn away from sin and toward God so we can run the race set before us in freedom.

Simply being sorry won't bring us peace. But sorrow?

The brokenness of sorrow brings us to the saving knowledge and grace of Jesus Christ and it's his forgiveness and kindness that lead us to repentance.

Stone Throwers and Coat Holders

I wouldn't say that I was one of the most popular kids in school. I was known as the pastor's kid, the religious character in the after-school television special who provided contrast and made good decisions. I did what I could to keep off the radar and avoid any unnecessary attention.

I can think of countless times I watched in the crowd as a fellow student—not so lucky to avoid attention—was picked on or mocked. If I had taken the risk to be brave and come to the rescue of someone being bullied, I figured I would then become the new target of those who loved fresh meat. My typical response was to stand in the back laughing to avoid attention turning to me. I didn't need to be the hero, but reflecting now, I see how hypocritical it was for me to be in seeming support of those inflicting pain on another person.

Our churches often function like high school.

For a blunter comparison: many Christians have picked up stones and thrown them at one another and many of us have held their coats.

In Acts, we see a similar display in the story of the stoning of Stephen.

Now in full stampede, they dragged him out of town and pelted him with rocks. *The ringleaders took off their coats and asked a young man named Saul to watch them.*

As the rocks rained down, Stephen prayed, "Master Jesus, take my life." Then he knelt down, praying loud enough for everyone to hear, "Master, don't blame them for this sin"—his last words. Then he died.

Saul was right there, congratulating the killers. (Acts 7:57–60 MSG)

Which is worse? Those persecuting people the Church should be protecting or those not willing to stop it?

Those causing the physical harm, those covering it up, or worse, those congratulating the people getting away with it?

I quoted Dr. Martin Luther King Jr. at the top of this chapter, and I believe it's worth repeating:

"It may well be that we will have to repent in this generation. Not merely for the vitriolic words and the violent actions of the bad people, but for the appalling silence and indifference of the good people who sit around and say, 'Wait on time.'"

One of the greatest examples we see of this in our churches today is the silence of those who knew leaders were sexually abusing someone and did nothing. Whatever their reasons—believing it was their job to just stay out of the way and not get involved, or not knowing what to do, or fear—the outcomes were the same to the victims. The silence of the coat holders is perceived as indifference and is just as painful and destructive as those throwing the stones; we find ourselves standing in the rubble of our churches due to the actions of both parties.

Are we sorry or sorrowful for those we have lost?

Where is the repentant heart of the Church for those we have broken?

Just as those in the Upper Room would come to repentance, we as the modern-day Church are also called to repent, not out of obligation, but from a deep desire to turn from our sin and run to Jesus. Only by the sacrifice Jesus made on the cross do we have access to the throne room to fall flat on our faces before the one true living God to ask for forgiveness. It's both a privilege and a responsibility, not just as leaders, but as Christ followers, to daily seek the grace of Jesus Christ.

The ground is level at the cross. There is no celebrity pastor, famous worship leader, or large-church staff who is without sin or exempt from the call to repentance.

We should model the power of repentance to those we lead and love. Every Sunday the Body of Christ should see their pastors and leaders modeling a humble and contrite heart at the feet of Jesus, especially when sin has been exposed at high levels of leadership.

I was recently with a good friend, reflecting about her own experiences with her church. She got unexpectedly pregnant at a young age and didn't marry the father, but rather than be a safehouse for a single mom with a brand-new baby, her church's response was whispers behind closed doors, awkward interactions, and backhanded compliments oozing with religious undertones. The pastor, whom she had known most of her life, didn't seem to know how to respond so he simply stopped pastoring her at all.

As we drove in the car together, I asked her what it would mean to hear her pastor say, even all these years later, "Please forgive me, I didn't handle that well at all," or something to that effect. The simple suggestion brought her to a quiet, tearful nod of "Yeah, that would be really nice."

For the next several days I thought about what true forgiveness means and how difficult it is to offer it to those who have left us scarred and bruised. Yet Jesus offers this same forgiveness to you and me every single day. I thought of Jesus on the cross and his words in Luke 23:34 when he said, "Father, forgive them, for they don't know what they are doing," hanging dying as an innocent man above soldiers gambling for his clothes. He had every right to be angry, hurt, to demand justice and make sure these men knew he was the Son of God, but the Scriptures tell us he "endured from sinners such hostility against himself" for the joy set before him (Heb. 12:3 ESV).

> Forgiveness will look different for each of us; we won't always get the resolution we seek or conversation we feel we deserve. But we can find peace in the release.

Though my friend doesn't attend this church on a regular basis or have a close relationship with the pastor, she is able to walk into the church with her head held high as a daughter of God. Forgiveness will look different for each of us; we won't always get the resolution we seek or conversation we feel we deserve. But we can find peace in the release. Forgiveness doesn't mean we give those who have hurt us access to us, it doesn't mean we have to trust them again. It simply means we have released them from the prison of our hearts so we can remain on this Kingdom-building mission of making disciples and sharing the Gospel of Jesus Christ without bitterness.

It means we no longer give those who have hurt us brain space. It means we can stop fighting invisible battles of the enemy in the shower—scheming someone's demise or saying things in our heads we'd never say in person—and instead use that time for dreaming with God.

Can you imagine if we, as individual people of the Church, humbled ourselves to say we weren't just sorry but were sorrowful for the hurt we caused someone and directly told them while we were still here on this earth and able to do this in person rather than at a memorial or graveside?

Our pews would be full! Prodigals would feel as if they were welcomed home without shame. Salvation would spring forth out of the dry mouths of those searching for living water.

Authentic testimonies would go from unheard to being shouted from the steepletop.

Corporate revival—rebuilding our churches—would follow individual repentance.

Our congregations are watching not only how we model repentance, but how we respond to those seeking forgiveness around us. Will we offer grace, mercy, kindness, compassion, and a safe place to heal?

Reflection Prayer

"Dear God, please forgive me for my sins: those in plain sight and those I have kept hidden. I repent of my sins, and I want to turn away from the sin that is entangling and weighing me down. Thank you for taking my place on the cross and bearing all my sin and shame. Forgive us as your Church for our sins, wash your Bride clean and make us new. We want to be your radiant Bride, healed and whole. Forgive us, Father. Help us to be more like you."

Chapter 10

WE WILL BE A HOUSE OF UNITY

Broken and Blessed

"And all the believers lived in a wonderful harmony, holding everything in common."

Acts 2:44 MSG

It doesn't get crazier than a church family. I say this with endearment because I was raised in equal parts by my biological family and my church family and both brought me love, many good memories, but also their own drama, scandals, and need for therapy.

I had outlandish church aunts who wore way too much red lipstick and rouge, boisterous church uncles who insisted on bringing squirrel chili to the chili cook-off (complete with the stories of how the squirrel was killed, and on whose property). I had church cousins who smoked behind the fellowship hall, persuaded me to be lookout as they made out with their church-camp crushes in the snack shack, and stayed up all night toilet papering church members' homes.

Nobody can love you and hurt you like your church family.

Because of my initials turned credentials ("P.K."), I have always felt an unspoken bond to every church I've served and attended. Everyone looks familiar, as if we've met in a former life, and there isn't a church person I can't find common ground with in under two seconds.

As it turns out, not every church family was ready to embrace their new little sister who came bouncing into their church community with Tigger from *Winnie-the-Pooh* force. It was a no-brainer for me: Hey! We work together now, we're family!

But it often feels as if there are more Eeyores than Tiggers in the family of God.

As a female worship pastor who worked primarily with men, I felt it was always important for me to make friends with the wives of those I served beside. I had seen so much division among worship teams because of unhealthy relationships between staff members and volunteers, so I made a point to at least take them out for coffee and get to know them as best I could.

In one particular staff assignment, I reached out to the worship pastor's wife and asked if I could take her to coffee. I wasn't looking to be her BFF. I didn't want to have sleepovers and braid each other's hair. In fact, it would have been much easier for me to just show up and start my job without any extra relational components because I'm not a BFF kind of a girl.

But I'll never forget hearing my phone beep, opening my text messages, and reading the words "No thank you, I have enough friends."

"No thank you, I have enough friends"?!

I have never felt my heart stop like it did in that moment. Not because I was rejected or desperate for friendship, but because I knew then I was stepping into a position where the foundation was more fragile and broken than I expected. This response had come from pain and recent woundedness that had nothing to do with me yet would affect my entire season with this team and house.

Divorce Court

The enemy's tired old tactic has always been to cause divorce within the family of God. He wants a broken home, a broken system, a dysfunctional unit that looks crazy to the rest of the world. You don't have to destroy a house if you can take out the family living inside.

Since the garden, Satan has been trying to keep us separated from God and one another. As we're seeing in the Western church, he doesn't have to try very hard. Church attendance continues to fall, pastors are resigning, and we're at each other's throats on topics ranging from politics to the color of carpet in the sanctuary.

As a lifetime member of the family of God, I can assure you that stiff-arming from the pastor's wife wasn't the first time I had been reminded of my place. Our churches, much like our biological families, have tables with assigned seats. And like a mistrustful family, sometimes you have to sit at the kiddie table for a bit to prove you're going to stick around longer than the last girl who just wanted to date their hot uncle.

There has been such high turnover—so many people coming and going from staff positions and congregations—and many have grown weary of the constant revolving door of ministry and church family. Why invest in someone if they are just going to leave? Why trust another leader if they are just going to hurt me like the others? We've been disappointed by those we love, and many of us are hesitant to jump back into a church family, or welcome others into ours, because of great loss and pain.

How often we find ourselves in church divorce court, sitting in offices signing NDAs, distributing assets, determining what is owned by the church or the individual, then parting ways with financial agreements and boundaries that feel sterile and impersonal. There are custody agreements: who gets what friends, who can start churches, and how many miles away they have to be so you don't steal from another family. It's an open-and-shut case nearly every time, those leaving are likely deemed divisive or off mission while those remaining are unclear why a family member is no longer at the table. We don't talk about it because we've never talked about it.

Through repentance and salvation we can learn how to be true brothers and sisters in Christ, how to have uncomfortable conversations while holding space for healing, restoration, and hopeful reconciliation.

God Loves His Family

Throughout the Bible, God clearly demonstrates his love for his kids and wants his family to work together for the building up of his Kingdom and one another. In Galatians 6:9–10, Paul writes, "So let's not get tired of doing what is good. At just the right time we will reap a harvest of blessing if we don't give up. Therefore, whenever we have the opportunity, we should do good to everyone—especially to those in the family of faith."

When the family of God cares for the family of God, we reap a harvest of blessing.

But if unity is what commands the Lord's blessing over a house, then the enemy will do everything he can to twist words, bring offense, and divide the house to bring chaos and confusion.

In most of the churches I travel to these days, I see church leaders attempting to take steps toward unity among their staff and congregation. But I sense exhaustion in their efforts as it is difficult to unify people who are diverse and divided on so many issues.

Think of the Thanksgiving or Christmas dinner conversation around the table with your own flesh and blood and the many topics that are either off limits or send Uncle Frank into a tailspin, red faced with bulging eyes. It can feel like even the most festive of occasions carries the potential for a bit of tension and uncertainty.

As pastors host panels on race, LGBTQ conversations, politics, church health, raising kids, and various issues in their cities, in their efforts to increase communication, they have no idea how what they had hoped would unify their house became more like a wrecking ball.

I can testify there are churches doing good Kingdom work hosting forums, community events, citywide projects, partnering with other local church families, and going into their Jerusalem and Judea and Samaria and the ends of the earth with hearts to see people back in a church family, even if it isn't their own. For as many shepherds who have hurt the sheep, there are thousands of other shepherds gently working to see the sheep restored and made whole.

It breaks my heart to sit across from these pastors and church leaders who tell me, "Natalie, we really thought we were doing good work and loving people where they are, and it's just not good enough. What are we doing wrong?"

And I don't have an answer for them. I still don't know how to respond to that question in the flesh. But in the spirit? I have my eyes on our enemy, a wolf in sheep's clothing roaming brazenly among the flock, and he wants to divide us. It's time we stop entertaining the liar among us.

The Earthquake of Offense

Christians might be the most offendable group of people on the planet.

When I was a little girl, I would hear people talking in the church hallways.

"Sister Mary left the church," they'd whisper. "She didn't get to sing her solo Sunday morning, so she took her tape and went up the street to the Baptist church."

As I grew up, I realized it didn't take much to offend a Christian. Satan doesn't have too many tricks up his sleeve, but we seem to fall for the same ones every time. It's like a game of telephone that spreads a disease through the hearts of even the healthiest believers until the cancer can't be cut out. We begin to see every decision, comment, sermon, and social media post as personal when in reality it had nothing to do with us.

If we're going to face off with the devil blowing hot air our way, we have to start building with the materials Jesus used to send him back where he belongs.

In Matthew chapter 4, Jesus had been in the desert fasting for forty days and nights. He was hungry and Satan showed up to tempt him with three things: food, proof of deity, and power. With each temptation, Jesus responded with Scripture.

When Satan tempted him to turn stones into bread, Jesus responded, "People do not live by bread alone, but by every word that comes from the mouth of God" (v. 4).

When Satan tempted him to prove he was God, Jesus responded, "The Scriptures also say, 'You must not test the LORD your God'" (v. 7).

When Satan tempted him with power, Jesus responded, "Get out of here, Satan ... For the Scriptures say, 'You must worship the LORD your God and serve only him'" (v. 10).

And I love verse 11, "Then the devil went away, and angels came and took care of Jesus."

Then the devil went away.

I speak this over you now: whatever offense the enemy is tempting you to carry, may you use the very Word of God as your foundation to build upon and the framework to build around your life. I speak freedom over your life: no longer wander in the desert of offense and anger toward people and situations but feast on the Bread of Life, who provides everything we need, even in barren seasons when it feels like the world is against us and the enemy after us.

My hope in writing this chapter is to challenge us as the people of the Church to stop falling for the same bait, to stand up to an enemy who would like nothing more than to see us self-destruct in our own mess. I want to be a Church who fights for each other, prays with one another, stands up to evil, and refuses to give the enemy access to our hearts and minds.

We're instructed to "carry each other's burdens" in Galatians 6:2 (NIV). In fact, this is "the law of Christ." But Christians seem to know how to pick up an offense better than they know how to bear a burden.

People are going to hurt us; our biological families as well as our church families will cancel us, critique us, and criticize our purest efforts. As Christ followers, we have to decide if we're going to let the enemy magnify the actions of a brother or sister to the point that we storm out of our house and refuse to open the door again, or refuse to step foot into another church family that might have something beautiful to offer us in the form of friendship and community.

Not only have we become weary carrying our own offense, but some of us are exhausted from carrying the offenses of others.

> **We can bear another's burdens without being buried by their offense.**

We have obsessed over people, situations, conversations, and outcomes that we have zero authority over and zero influence to change. How often we enter another person's race when we can barely run our own. We must stop picking up weapons for war on territory where we have no assignment and there is no battle to be fought. It's a good way to get hurt because we don't have cover or permission to be there.

We can pray for those hurting whether from our prayer closet, fighting on our knees, or interceding in worship. People will want us to take sides, but our loyalty is to one Kingdom holding only what is placed in our hands.

We can bear another's burdens without being buried by their offense. Proverbs 18:19 says, "A brother offended is more unyielding than a strong city, and quarreling is like the bars of a castle" (ESV).

Jesus tells us to bear one another's burdens, but he never tells us to carry offenses—those committed against us or others. One is just dead weight, but the other a burden he wants to carry with us. If we are to be a unified house, a Church who cannot be divided, we must lay down our offenses at the foot of the cross.

The Growth of the Church Is the Grief of the Enemy

Not only has Satan been trying to divorce God's Church, but he has also been out to kill, steal, and destroy every member of God's family. Why?

Because the growth of the Kingdom of God threatens his kingdom of darkness. He doesn't have too many creative strategies, and as we take a deeper look into the Scriptures, we can see his plans for demolition lack power or effectiveness against God's Church.

In Exodus we meet Pharaoh, who was terrified God's people would outnumber and overpower the Egyptians.

"He said to his people, 'Look, the people of Israel now outnumber us and are stronger than we are. We must make a plan to keep them from growing even more. If we don't, and if war breaks out, they will join our enemies and fight against us. Then they will escape from our country'" (1:9–10).

In his attempts to control the situation, Pharaoh made sure the Israelites depended on him, as he enslaved them and killed anyone who threatened his position and power. He did everything in his power to limit the growth of the Israelites.

> So the Egyptians made the Israelites their slaves. They appointed brutal slave drivers over them, hoping to wear them down with crushing labor. They forced them to build the cities of Pithom and Rameses as supply centers for the king. But the more the Egyptians oppressed them, the more the Israelites multiplied and spread, and the more alarmed the Egyptians became. So the Egyptians worked the people of Israel without mercy. They made their lives bitter, forcing them to mix mortar and make bricks and do all the work in the fields. They were ruthless in all their demands. (vv. 11–14)

To keep the Israelites from being fruitful, Pharaoh wanted to stop them from reproducing. He demanded that two female midwives kill any Hebrew baby boys born in their presence: "When you help the Hebrew women as they give birth, watch as they deliver. If the baby is a boy, kill him; if it is a girl, let her live" (v. 16). Thankfully, the two midwives, named Shiphrah and Puah, were friends of God and worked quickly to ensure the boys were delivered healthy and safe.

Satan is doing everything in his power to limit the growth of our churches and is not much different in his attempts.

Satan's strategy to destroy our churches:

- He gaslights our churches into thinking we are poor and powerless.
- He convinces us we are slaves to our sin.
- He tries to break our spirit and divide us from within.
- He comes after our marriages and our children.
- He discourages us from entering covenant with God.
- He wears down our physical and mental health in numerous ways.
- He encourages us to destruct and detach from God and one another and align ourselves with the world, or better yet, be isolated with him.

Although Pharaoh had a strategy, the midwives had a strategy, or focus, of their own:

- They feared God more than Pharaoh.
- They came when called even though it was risky.
- They knew where their identity came from and remained steadfast in that truth.
- They chose to allow God to use them to help protect the innocent lives of the baby boys.

Much like the midwives who rescued the baby boys, we have an opportunity as churches, but we need a strategy:

- We fear God more than man—or the enemy.
- We sit by one another and hand deliver what God is birthing through us—individually and as a family.
- We allow God to use us, even in our weakness and humanity, to love, serve, and rescue his people.

The Scriptures tell us that God dealt well with the midwives. "So God was good to the midwives, and the Israelites continued to multiply, growing more and more powerful. And because the midwives feared God, he gave them families of their own" (Ex. 1:20–21).

We are all vital parts of the family of God. There are no favorites. He loves us all with an unwavering love and he will use us, the least powerful, to partner with him to grow his Church if we will unify to fight off the evil one.

Let me take some pressure off here: We do not have to build God's Church. God is perfectly capable of building his Church. He has laid the foundation; we're just reviewing what the blueprints we find in his Word are telling us. We are called to disciple and love those in our churches. If we are willing to raise our own children—biological and spiritual children alike—God will grow his Church and build us into families. He will bless our children and prosper them in all they do. Because we have protected and stood beside one another, God will make us his Church and establish a family for us to worship with until his return.

It won't be a perfect family, but it will be beautiful.

The Fight for Unity

As I spent more time in the first few chapters of Acts, I found many similarities to my own upbringing in the local church. Yes, I had seen a lot of hurt and confusion among the saints, but I also found a family. That family has gone from our small churches in the Midwest to a global church family through the Raised to Stay online community. As messy as we are, we are family.

In Acts 2:46–47, we learn more about the early Church.

"They followed a daily discipline of worship in the Temple followed by meals at home, every meal a celebration, exuberant and joyful, as they praised God. People in general liked what they saw. Every day their number grew as God added those who were saved" (MSG).

The unity of the first church family was fought for by their commitment to show up to the Temple every single day to worship. Not just on Sundays, not just when they were scheduled on Planning Center, but every day. Following each time of worship they shared a meal, not simply tolerating one another, but in celebration as they broke bread and praised God.

Notice here, "People in general liked what they saw" (v. 47).

In other words, the general public was drawn to the unity they were witnessing from afar and as a result, "Every day their number grew as God added those who were saved" (v. 47).

I can already see you rolling your eyes. Natalie, we don't have time to go to church every day. It's a different era. You can't possibly be suggesting we need to host worship nights every single night of the week.

You are right. It's a different time and a different day and I don't believe we have to gather every night of every week to see unity in our church family.

I am not suggesting we host a conference that requires every ounce of energy of our church staff and volunteers to execute with perfection. I am not asking us to wear out marketing departments and communications teams by making graphics and social media content. I am not saying we need to bring in a megachurch evangelist or a famous worship band to help bring in the masses. That isn't unity.

However, I do believe we can:

- Commit to showing up when the doors are open on a unified mission of the Holy Spirit, not out of obligation, but with a sense of expectation.
- Arrive a few minutes early on Sunday mornings to pray over chairs, to welcome a visitor, to take a family on a tour of the kids' ministry, to grab a cup of coffee with a congregant.
- Stop running on empty trying to be all things to all people. Slow down long enough to actually make eye contact with those we serve—perhaps even have an intentional conversation.

I am asking for every member of the church staff to attend the church-wide prayer meeting when called by leadership.

I am asking for every member of the church staff to be at the staff meeting regardless of your title or position.

I am asking for every congregant to make Sundays and other weekly services a priority, not an afterthought.

Because something special happens when the family of God gathers.

The world is watching. If we're going to have social media, let's start posting photos of what happens among us at our big tables when we break bread: laughing, hugging, and sharing in real life.

These watching people, in addition to our own church people, are desperate for an authentic community where they can come as they are and find family. The beauty of the early Church wasn't their perfection or policies, it was their posture for more of the Holy Spirit and their willingness to welcome others, sharing in everything.

I am often asked: How do we fight for unity in our churches when we don't have a major role in leadership or any power to influence or make decisions? I know it can be frustrating to see areas for potential change but feel as if our hands are tied. It's not as dire as we often feel when we look around and think there's nothing to be done at the level we find ourselves.

When I was a young worship leader learning to navigate the intimidating world of Christian songwriting, my friend Krissy Nordhoff, an award-winning songwriter and mentor of other worship leaders and songwriters, taught me a lesson I'll never forget:

> *If I want to see change in my church or ministry,*
> ***be what I needed*** *when I was first starting out in*
> *ministry, on a church staff, or in a church.*

Did you need a mentor? Be a mentor.

Did you need a safe place to process big questions? Be willing to answer questions.

Did you need someone to take you to coffee when you were new? Keep a few dates in your calendar open.

Did you need someone to disciple you? Watch for those God places on your heart to lead.

Many of us began ministry on our own and figured things out the hard way through failing, and sometimes even quitting, because we didn't have the support we needed to succeed at our roles. When we step into these roles for the next generation, we are already establishing a foundation that is stronger than the one we first stepped out onto.

Church, it doesn't matter if our buildings are pretty on the outside if we are ugly and disjointed in the way we relate to each other on the inside. People are no longer impressed by suits and status; they would rather know us at our worst than fake know us and be kept at a distance. Sometimes unity looks like ripped jeans on a Sunday morning, messy buns at Bible study, and awkward parenting advice.

People are okay with the worship leader losing a lyric, a missed slide during the sermon, coffee stains on our shirts and lipstick on our teeth. People like messy because in so many ways messiness unifies humanity. They want a church they can live in and a Kingdom family they can live with, not a place to be

> **People like messy because in so many ways messiness unifies humanity.**

entertained by well-dressed performers who know a script but don't know their name.

They want to see us laugh and cry, play and rest, worship and lament. They want all of us, not just the good days, but the bad ones too. They want our humanity and the anointing, and when we're lucky the two collide. Because it's there they find Jesus, the true power behind the persona, the hope behind the hype, the truth behind the smoke and mirrors.

They don't want magical, they want tangible. They want leaders they can follow and voices they can trust and shoulders to cry on and necks to hug and ears that will listen and hands they can hold. They don't want what we do, they want us.

They want a broken Church who knows how to build from the rubble and understands the role of a remnant, who knows what to do with leftovers. They are looking for our creativity, innovation, and above all, love. This world doesn't need a pretty Church. It needs a holy Church.

A sanctified Church.

An honest Church.

A repenting Church.

A godly Church.

And as 1 Corinthians 3:16 reminds us, that Church is found in you and me.

"You realize, don't you, that you are the temple of God, and God himself is present in you? No one will get by with vandalizing God's temple, you can be sure of that. God's temple is sacred—and you, remember, *are* the temple" (MSG).

No Man Left Behind

When Peter stood up in Acts chapter 2 and began preaching to those skeptical of what they had witnessed, he had the backing of the remaining disciples. After they witnessed this beautiful outpouring of the Holy Spirit, questions of what's next emerged. Peter didn't hesitate to give them their marching orders, and the other apostles were right there to support him.

He unapologetically shared the Gospel, ending his message with a bold statement: "So let everyone in Israel know for certain that God has made this Jesus, whom you crucified, to be both Lord and Messiah!" (Acts 2:36).

The people seemed to appreciate his direct delivery; they didn't stomp out offended or ask for another disciple to explain it. Instead they asked Peter and the disciples, "Brothers, what should we do?" (v. 37).

Peter then laid out the clear path for building the very first church starting with two key components: repentance and baptism. Luke tells us that three thousand people were added that day. But it didn't stop there. The people continued to listen to the teachings of the apostles: "And all the believers lived in a wonderful harmony, holding everything in common" (v. 44 MSG).

Thankfully, Peter had the backing of the others (in addition to the Holy Spirit). We have sent good people in to do hard things and didn't back them up when they needed us because we forgot self-preservation isn't a fruit of the Holy Spirit.

I have been on enough church staff teams to know how many Peters we leave hanging who are speaking up on behalf of others. We complain and commiserate over lunch, all raising similar concerns about a particular leader or decision and we send a poor soul in who is willing to speak up only to wimp out when it comes our turn to use our voices.

People are looking for strong leadership from godly leaders, those who are willing to give them hard truth in love. As leaders, consistent, unified communication in our churches is not only a strong tool for rebuilding a solid foundation but a valuable weapon against the tired tools of the enemy, such as offense and confusion.

What does healthy communication bring to our churches?

Good communication invites encouragement, affirmation, and correction and provides protection from misunderstandings and vain imaginations. It welcomes hard and holy conversations and brings false assumptions into the light, establishing godly order and paralyzing an enemy hell-bent on causing chaos and confusion in the family of God.

Godly counsel, mentorship, and discipleship provide tools for development and growth—weapons to protect the hearts of the next generation learning how to go into battle as the unified Church. Avoiding hard conversations doesn't equip or protect anyone. One of the greatest gifts we can give and receive is modeling relationship that reveals the heart of the Father and a deep love for one another.

> **Avoiding hard conversations doesn't equip or protect anyone.**

In the day-to-day, timely responses to emails, keeping scheduled one-on-ones and meetings with colleagues, and offering honest feedback and expectations minister to those we lead and model wise stewardship of time and people. As leaders, excusing poor communication on our Enneagram number or personality type is irresponsible. It is not good leadership to assume our content, art, position, and title do the talking for us.

At its worst, bad communication can hurt people and create discord among the family of God. I have seen leaders simply refuse to grow in their communication skills but then leave a wake of bodies behind them who didn't survive their leadership style. In an unhealthy season, failure to connect with those entrusted to us could be a form of spiritual abuse.

If you aren't good at communication, take some courses and find a mentor as soon as possible. We can all learn how to be better; it is a lifelong process. Good leaders learn and wise leaders know how to be led.

The enemy thrives on chaos.

Our God establishes order.

Our message and skills are gifts we have been given that place us in our roles as leaders. It is our responsibility to then love one another well, and one way we do that is through clear and conscientious communication. Clarity is kindness.

Steward your interactions with people as if you were preparing a sermon or worship set for thousands; it is that important in building healthy cultures in God's Church.

The Beautiful Ministry of Listening

Perhaps the best way to communicate well with others may be the hardest for some of us in leadership: listening.

So many misunderstandings happen in the family of God because we are quick to want to be heard but lack the discipline of listening.

The best kept secret in ministry are the listeners. Those who understand the art of the holy hush.

A lot of people in our churches know how to talk and expect to be heard, but few know how to sit in the tension of what has yet to be said. This is where our ears do the work, our hearts do the under-standing, and our souls become sacred spaces and secret keepers as the Holy Spirit slows us down to give us the next steps. Do we give advice? Do we ask them if we can pray for them? Do we offer to help them find a counselor? This is where we empathize but don't try to fix anything or defend anyone because talk can be cheap.

Don't ever discount the equity we gain by opening our ears and closing our mouths. People don't necessarily want answers—and you won't always have words to say—they just want to know they are heard. As the family of God we must learn to lean into one another, it's easy to drown out the whispers of those in need when we feel the need to always have an answer.

Listening costs the hearer the comfort of their own voice.

In listening, we introduce others to a God who hears.

This same God longs for his family to find unity in all the noise, joined together in his name for his purpose.

Let it start with us.

Reflection Prayer

"Dear God, unify your Church for your glory. Bring us together as one, in one accord, unified by mission and the promise of your

Holy Spirit. Forgive me for carrying offenses, reveal to me any area where I still have unresolved offense so I can lay it down. Draw us together as your family—brothers and sisters who will love and serve one another and not allow anything of the enemy to divide us. Bind us together in your Name to be the family so many are desperate to find."

Chapter 11

WE WILL BE A HOUSE OF REVIVAL

Restoration and Renewal

*"And each day the Lord added to their fellowship
those who were being saved."*

Acts 2:47

When I share my testimony of growing up in the local church, you
will often hear me mention revival services as core memories from
my adolescence. These scheduled weeklong gatherings took place
several times a year in churches, under tents, or in convention cen-
ters. I looked forward to them each time, knowing I'd see old friends
and be among those who also loved worshipping Jesus.

I learned from experience that when the people of God came
together for a concentrated time of prayer, worship, fasting, and
community, anything could happen. I witnessed with my own
eyes physical healings, the return of long-lost prodigals, marriages

restored, and so many other miraculous moments—not because a bunch of church people planned an event, but because unified saints intentionally gathered in an Upper Room and waited on the Holy Spirit to move among them.

And he did.

The Merriam-Webster Dictionary defines *revival* as "an act or instance of reviving: the state of being revived: such as a renewed attention to or interest in something, a new presentation or publication of something old, a period of renewed religious interest, an often highly emotional evangelistic meeting or series of meetings."[9]

The Church is a historical, living, breathing organism with a metaphorical foundation and cornerstone laid by Jesus with a structure of strong stones added by the apostles. The first gathering of believers that hosted the arrival of the Holy Spirit—leading to the belief and baptism of thousands and the birth of the Church—consisted of:

- prayer
- unity
- worship
- commitment to finish
- message and mission centered on Jesus Christ
- repentance
- forgiveness
- community
- lives of surrender and sacrifice

When I look at the definition of *revival* and then compare it to what happened in the Upper Room, I get excited! "A renewed attention to or interest in something, a new presentation or publication of something old."

Is it possible that churches spend their time and resources planning revivals and conferences with the hope of getting as many people into one place as possible, not for show, but because God is calling us to a renewed attention to and interest in the foundational, biblical building blocks of his Church? He is calling us as his Bride back to prayer, unity, worship, finishing what we start, the message and mission of Jesus Christ, repentance, forgiveness, community, and surrender.

Those revivals from my childhood weren't just nostalgia, though I'm thankful God will sometimes use nostalgia to bring us back to an old church home or community, even if for just one service or a holiday. I went to those revivals expecting the Holy Spirit to not only show up but to move among us with power and purpose, and I left different because I encountered the Living God surrounded by the family of God.

Over the past several years I have had dreams where the Holy Spirit has given me scriptures and strategy regarding his Church and those serving his Church. I am careful about what dreams or visions I share, knowing some are meant to stay between me and God while others are more of a corporate word for the Body of Christ.

Recently, I got brave enough to share one of my dreams with the Raised to Stay online family and the comments came pouring in from other believers who were having similar dreams and revelation from the Lord. I love how God is intentional with us, giving us prophetic wisdom through his Word to guide us in the process of continuing to build his Kingdom and serve his Church.

Just as Jesus carefully gave final instructions to the disciples and those in the room with him before he ascended into heaven, we have been left with the same mandate and promise of the Holy Spirit to help us.

More Than a Movement

The Old Testament is filled with stories where we find elements of "revival" or "renewal," as ordinary men and women put their extraordinary God on display. From Elijah to Hezekiah, even Jonah preaching in Nineveh, we see how the Holy Spirit shows up among his people when they are willing to make God's glory known even in their own difficult circumstances.

The revival on Pentecost Sunday brought great growth and multiplication to the first Church with three thousand being baptized in one day. This was the beginning of what we now know as the Church, and we can follow the apostles through the entire book of Acts as they were obedient to preach the Gospel of Jesus Christ. From Philip's ministry to the Samaritans to Luke, Paul, and Silas at the house of Lydia and eventually into the house of the jailer, to the women who opened their homes and businesses, it took all hands on deck to see the message of Jesus Christ taken to the far ends of the earth.

Ray Stedman wrote that the book of Acts is "a tremendous record of apostolic success," and anything that finds success is at risk of being imitated, primarily the faults over the virtues.[10]

How quick we Christians chase movements and imitate what has worked for the generations before us. We see what has worked for other churches or organizations and quickly slap our logo on something that was never ours to own, it was a borrowed vision that may or may not align with our mission or values as a church.

I've heard it said that imitation is the greatest form of flattery, but in some cases it's plagiarism or theft. When God asks us to build something, he will never ask us to steal materials from another person's house. The only place we will find everything we need to build anything lasting in God's name is in his blueprint, the Word of God.

When my youngest daughter was seven, she discovered Legos and became a little architect (if I do say so myself). She loved to build things from scratch, and I get that because we're creators made in the image of God, and I'm learning that my role in the Kingdom is to build things for the Church with my friends.

Occasionally she would get frustrated because to finish her project she needed a specific piece. And the very piece she needed was usually embedded in my house as part of the foundation.

I would try to explain that I wasn't going to disassemble my house just so she could have that one piece she needed, but I would show her creative ways to make a long piece using a few smaller pieces. Sometimes she would get creative but other times she just destroyed it all and quit.

All my life I've watched laborers in Christ build things together and then break off to begin something new. And I'm always fascinated by the leaders who can take nothing and make something from it using God-given materials, funds, and co-laborers.

There were times people would lend materials and share pieces as they helped one another build. Like when I would hand off a brick to my daughter because I wanted to help her get started.

But other times people would steal resources from another house because they got started and realized they were missing a piece. Rather than getting resourceful, they stole from another man's house. They went from being a builder to being a thief.

No good house can stand on a stolen foundation.

Shared resources and stolen resources will build two very different structures. If the Lord has called you to build something, he will never ask you to steal from another man's house. He will provide, he will equip, he will bring co-laborers called to your assignment.

With each new ministry and assignment, we form relationships and learn how to steward what we've been given. We trust God for the resources as we protect the people.

No Recipe for Revival

For many of us from traditional backgrounds (as I shared from most of my childhood), revival has always meant a week of long nights at our church, the women in their pretty dresses and the men wearing fresh pressed suits. We showed up to give God our best and scheduled to do it again the same week the following year.

Until that antiquated perception was blown one night in February 2023. As I was getting ready for bed, I heard on the news about a spontaneous and public revival that had broken out on a college campus.

For nearly a month our nation was captivated by an unplanned revival that broke out during a normal Wednesday-morning chapel service at Asbury University, a small Christian college in an even smaller Kentucky town. News of the revival spread around the world with those coming from as far away as Japan to Wilmore,

Kentucky, to see firsthand what God was doing among the faculty and students. With lines wrapped through buildings and down streets, people traveled hours to stand even longer in snow and rain to witness this outpouring of the Holy Spirit in a modern-day Upper Room.

It wasn't on the school calendar, there weren't any slick marketing campaigns or social media posts, students simply went into a room like they did every Wednesday morning, and they were changed by the power of the Holy Spirit.

For several weeks people came from far and wide by planes and cars to witness in person what they were seeing online. I believe we all want to be part of a movement of God. We sing about it and pray for it, and we want to experience the power of God for ourselves.

How encouraging it is to know God can choose to anoint everyday people anywhere in the world to lead people with authority and excellence every single day. He doesn't need us, but what an honor it is that he chooses us to partner with him in this Kingdom work.

Revival isn't prescriptive; it doesn't always come with a Planning Center invite or offer us a week to get ready. Revival can be student led or parent run. It can break out during a Celebrate Recovery meeting or in the kitchen among a few exhausted moms looking for more of Jesus.

> We may not get a say in where or how revival falls, but we can be positioned for it to fall on us.

We may not get a say in where or how revival falls, but we can be positioned for it to fall on us.

He chose Asbury just as he will choose shepherd boys to be kings.

He can choose any one of us.

And to that I pray, Holy Spirit, come.

We Don't Have to Chase Revival

As news of the Asbury revival spread like wildfire across social media and news outlets, Christians around the world felt an urgent need to get there as soon as possible to witness revival in action. As I watched my brothers and sisters in Kentucky experience a mighty move of God from Colorado, I too wanted to pack up my car and drive toward the fire, but the Lord reminded me that I carry my own flame. And if I will stir it up, he will light it up; I don't have to drive fifteen hundred miles to find revival. Don't get me wrong, if God tells us to go somewhere and participate in a move of the Holy Spirit, we shouldn't hesitate to act out of obedience and go, but here's what I pray we all discover:

God will move in our city just as mightily as he moved in Asbury and all the other places revival has fallen since that day in the Upper Room.

Other college campuses throughout the United States and around the world began to see similar outpourings of the Holy Spirit. Some thought it was ingenuine, as if there were a magic code to revival someone had just helped them crack, but I was encouraged to see students taking initiative to lead their peers and press into the presence of God with fervency. Though they didn't last nearly as long or gain as much media presence, those who pursued the presence of God encountered the Living God and that is beautiful.

What if we didn't load up buses to drive to another city and instead filled the churches and college campuses in our towns with worship and prayer? What if we opened our homes and schools and cafes to the people we walk among every day and introduced them to a move of God?

I was convicted at how quickly I wanted to chase after the power of God when that same power moves and lives in me. Why are we so drawn to movements and expressions that can be joined or captured rather than our own mission right in front of us? Maybe it's because we're desperate for a move of God in our own lives but we've grown dry and weary where we are. It's too hard to build from scratch; we'd rather take someone else's Lego.

Cities aren't magical and movements aren't forever, so we must learn to fan the flame within us and be the light in the darkness around us. So, be it. Do it. Start it. Don't chase revival, pursue the power of God. What he has done at Asbury and other churches around the globe he will do for us all because he loves to meet with his people.

> **Movements aren't forever, so we must learn to fan the flame within us and be the light in the darkness around us.**

As we step out in obedience, with Christ as our foundation and the framework materials of worship, prayer, serving, and community in our blueprint, we will build a Church that is not only hospitable to the lost but also created for revival.

Holy Spirit, Come

I'm at a place where I can pray for revival in every church, even those where I have been hurt and disappointed, but it has taken me years of healing, pursuing spiritual direction by spending time in God's presence, the continual process of repentance, and seeking reconciliation and restoration with brothers and sisters in Christ. Maybe you aren't there yet, but God's healing is for us all. Psalm 147:3 tells us, "He heals the brokenhearted and bandages their wounds."

Prior to the revival that fell in the Upper Room, the eleven remaining disciples, along with Mary and Jesus' brothers, were found in Jerusalem right where Jesus told them to go, waiting for the promised gift of the Holy Spirit. Jesus spoke for the last time in Acts chapter 1, giving them their final orders to take the message of salvation near, far, and to the ends of the earth. The disciples watched as he ascended into heaven, leaving them to finish what they had begun together.

Then Peter pointed out the elephant in the room: it was time to replace Judas, the one who had betrayed Jesus and died. We have no idea how that conversation went, but we do know that right before the Holy Spirit came into the Upper Room, Judas was replaced by Matthias after much prayer and the very reliable drawing of straws.

When I think back to the Judas figures in my life, I can see how I allowed their presence or even their memory to stifle me and keep me from renewing my heart. I have been bitter; I have grown weary in waiting for an apology and it has felt impossible to move on or move forward when the hurt is still so fresh.

Revival fell in Acts 2 because God promised the Holy Spirit was coming, and it fell on imperfect people who were most likely still processing pain. But they didn't leave; they were in the room. They stayed in position and waited as Jesus had instructed because they believed that when Jesus said something, he meant it.

As I visit churches, young adult gatherings, universities, and conferences, I am praying for true revival. I am coming with fire shut up in my bones. I am believing that if we can fix our eyes on Jesus, our firm foundation, and lock eyes with him, we won't become so easily distracted by the enemy's schemes. We will withstand the storms and hot breath of an adversary who is old and tired.

I don't want any of us to miss out on true personal or corporate revival.

We need revival more than we need revenge. I believe the kindness of our good Father leads to repentance, and forgiveness is close behind. We can't waste precious time planning retaliation when we could be on our knees seeking restoration in the family of God.

We should thirst more for righteousness than we thirst to be right. Where is our desperation for an Upper Room movement? We don't need the upper hand. Will we come together and wait in expectation for an outpouring of the Holy Spirit rather than focusing our efforts on outing or ousting others? Will we contend for unity in our churches, for multiplication and addition? Will we choose to count our blessings rather than calculating faults and failures of leaders, churches, and pastors?

Will we be more interested in building with God than we are tearing people down? Will we focus our efforts on building our lives on Jesus, our right and true foundation, because whatever is built in alignment with him will be right and true too? What a shame it would be to live our lives waiting for people or organizations to fail or fall.

Are we ready to stop blaming the Church so we can be the Church?

Are we ready to stop blaming the Church so we can be the Church?

I am waiting and watching with hopeful anticipation that we will see his Kingdom come on earth as it is in heaven.

I lay down my rights.

I lay down my pride.

Holy Spirit, come.

Fill your churches with your Spirit.

Reflection Prayer

"Dear God, bring revival and renewal to your Church and your people. Come like a mighty rushing wind into each church, staff, volunteer team meeting, and prayer group as your sons and daughters gather to worship, pray, and spend time in your Word. Bring revival into our homes, schools, workplaces, and let it begin with personal revival in my own heart and life. Holy Spirit, fall fresh on me. I will remain until you come."

Chapter 12

WE ARE THE HOUSE OF THE REMNANT

Radical and Redeemed

"'In the last days,' God says, 'I will pour out my Spirit upon all people. Your sons and daughters will prophesy. Your young men will see visions, and your old men will dream dreams. In those days I will pour out my Spirit even on my servants—men and women alike—and they will prophesy.'"

Acts 2:17–18

The first section of this book introduced *rubblization*, a process in construction in which builders take unwanted concrete and break it down into small pieces that are used in the base for new surfaces.

I have good news for all of us. God is scooping up the destroyed, broken pieces of our faulty foundation that has crumbled beneath us and he's going to do something beautiful with it. Best of all: he wants us there building with him.

The Church is God's chosen remnant, built up with the living stones that are you and me only through the power of the Holy Spirit and the Word of God. Peter and the other apostles were among the first to lay the foundation of the Church, which is why their names will be written in the foundations of the new Jerusalem: "The wall of the city had twelve foundation stones, and on them were written the names of the twelve apostles of the Lamb" (Rev. 21:14).

> We are a radical remnant of those who believe we are called to build something beautiful in the rubble even though we've come close to walking away.

You and I are among those laying foundational stones today, as the radical remains of God's Church.

The word *remnant* is defined as "a usually small part, member, or trace remaining; a small surviving group—often used in plural."[11]

The *Anchor Bible Dictionary* describes a *remnant* as "what is left of a community after it undergoes a catastrophe."[12]

Throughout the Bible are stories introducing us to those who have remained after extreme catastrophe, such as Noah and his family, the remnant of the flood in Genesis 6. There was Elijah to whom God promised a remnant of seven thousand would join him in not bowing to idols in 1 Kings 19. Only Lot and his daughters survived the destruction of Sodom and Gomorrah in Genesis 19.

And now you and I remain scattered throughout the sanctuaries of our churches, loving God's people the best we know how. We are a radical remnant of those who believe we are called to build something beautiful in the rubble even though we've come close to walking away.

What makes us *radical*? The original definition of this word might surprise you.

> *Radical* comes from a Latin word meaning "root," and in its earliest uses it referred to roots of various kinds, first literal and then figurative. Because roots are the deepest part of a plant, *radical* came to describe things understood as fundamental or essential.[13]

We are radical because we are rooted and established in Christ, his Word being foundational and essential to our everyday lives as we take up our crosses and follow him.

"And now, just as you accepted Christ Jesus as your Lord, you must continue to follow him. Let your roots grow down into him, and let your lives be built on him. Then your faith will grow strong in the truth you were taught, and you will overflow with thankfulness" (Col. 2:6–7).

Here's what I've learned about staying from following Jesus and loving his Church:

- We will want to quit a little every day. We will ask the
  Lord to take this thorn from our flesh, to let the cup

pass us by; we will ask for the cross to be lighter and the burden to be lifted. We will beg for friends who will tarry with us for just a few moments longer as we face unimaginable pain, loss, and unknowns. They may or may not, but Jesus Christ will always be with us.

- There will be days we are tempted to call down ten thousand angels to our rescue, but Jesus demonstrated endurance for the joy set before him. That joy wasn't his own reputation but our salvation, so watch the Savior closely. Eyes up. Arms wide. Voice strong.

- We will be betrayed by friends and foes, but when he was betrayed, Jesus welcomed a thief into his Kingdom. In his humiliation, he scorned shame. Oh hell, where is your victory, oh death where is your sting? Observe your King, who didn't try to save himself but stayed to save you and me.

- You only get an empty tomb if you're willing to be buried. In his resurrection, Jesus got up and got out, rolling rocks, shaking ground. And that's the scary part, trusting the promises of God like the disciples did in the Upper Room—that he will show up on the other side of suffering.

- I know you're tired: come all who are weary. I know you are worn: come all who are heavy laden. Following Jesus comes with a cross but ends in a resurrection; stay in position. Hold on just one more day, for joy comes in the morning and you're almost through the night.

The Church might be bruised, it might have taken a beating, but it isn't broken.

You may be bruised, you may have taken a beating, but even in your brokenness, God is making something beautiful.

The Remnant: Both Male and Female

"'In the last days,' God says, 'I will pour out my Spirit upon all people. Your sons and daughters will prophesy'" (Acts 2:17).

As I'm a woman who carries the title *pastor*, as well as being a Christian female content creator and author, you can only imagine the comments I receive about where people feel women belong in the Church. I tend to ignore most of the trolls and bless and block. I love order in the Church, I believe in order in the Church, but I also believe women are foundational pieces to the radical remnant and the new foundation we're laying as we return to God and rebuild with him.

Women, you are one of God's best ideas. He created you with intentionality and great purpose. He assigned some of his most precious attributes to you and is unapologetic in how he formed you. You carry his gentle fire, meek authority, patient endurance, and discerning heart. He didn't forget to make you a man; he is quite sure of you and knew what he was doing when he made you a woman.

You have been given access to special areas of your Father's heart. As his daughter, you lack nothing yet give all you have because generosity and hospitality have been woven into your veins. You don't have to compete or compare, because you have your own DNA, delicately designed to carry out a mission so unique that all of heaven watches.

Your voice moves the heart of God and makes hell tremble, so speak loudly, pray louder. Use what you've been given and then dare to ask for more. Carry what you've been given with passionate grace and take with you those entrusted to your assignment.

Lead with wisdom and battle with intercession.

The Young Remnant

As a pastor's kid, I wouldn't say I thrived in the Church growing up, but I certainly survived it. Now my husband and I are doing the best we can to raise our own children in the Church with a new set of challenges this generation faces. My parents were pretty amazing at protecting my sister and me but even their best attempts couldn't shield us from church hurt and our own personal faith struggles. We all face things at some point, and thank you, Jesus, for your grace!

As my husband and I raise our own teenage daughters in the church, we, too, find ourselves winging it with the help of mentors and grandparents and pastors. It's a daily endeavor to teach our kids to love God and love people—even when the people are ridiculously people-y.

Here are some ways we can guide our children and this next generation as they develop their own relationships with the Church and church people:

- We acknowledge the unhealthy behaviors we see in leadership or church culture as a family with both honor and honesty. We honor the House of God while also teaching them how to discern what they sense from the Holy Spirit and how to use their voices to express concern.

- We don't gaslight them or defend behavior that makes them uncomfortable. If they don't want to go to youth group or a church event, we ask questions that turn to wonder. We ask ourselves, *I wonder what has been said or done, or not said or not done, to make them disengage.*

- We are mindful of how they hear us speak about sensitive church topics, leaders, and congregants. Their young ears might be able to process the information, but their hearts and minds are still developing. You might hear people call Christian kids "old souls," but they are still developing and growing in their discernment.

- We don't force them into discipleship, mentorship, or friendship with anyone they aren't comfortable being around. If they say no, we respect their decision and continue to pray for trusted voices to speak into their lives.

- We go to church as a family in the main sanctuary as often as possible. We want them to see us worship and encounter God as we engage in the service with our church family.

- We put them to work. One Sunday a month they work in a kids' ministry, greet, serve coffee, or pray at the altars with others. We are trying to teach them how to fall in love with the people in the church rather than any position or title. We want them to look people in the eyes, know their names, and seek them out again the next week.

- We teach intentional rest and Sabbath, especially in busy seasons of ministry and work. We want them to develop healthy rhythms now to set them up for success as adults.

- We keep conversations open in our home; nothing is off topic. No sin is too great, nothing needs to be hidden, and nobody needs to be shamed. We confess. We forgive. We pursue Jesus above all—not perfection.

- We let them know they mean more to us than church life. In the past that has meant leaving a church, letting them go to a different church, and defending them when they have been mistreated.

Our children are our first ministry. They are our greatest Kingdom legacy, a large part of the Church's floorplan and this radical remnant.

The Hidden Remnant

I love how we started this book talking about the temptation to build man-made castles on shifting sand and we're ending this book celebrating a remnant: those who have lived their lives as servants of Christ in hidden places, building the Kingdom with the Rock of ages. Isaiah 26:4–5 says, "Trust in ADONAI forever, for the LORD ADONAI is a Rock of ages. For He humbles those dwelling on high, leveling the lofty city, leveling it to the ground, bringing it down to the dust" (TLV).

Of the 120 in the Upper Room that morning, only eleven had recognizable names. There were a few others we may have known, but most were unknown. God said he would pour out his Spirit on his servants, and that, Church, is me and you.

The unrecognizable ones. Kingdom builders don't build for earthly recognition but rather for eternal echoes. You know nothing you have is yours to keep, nothing taken ever belonged to you. It is his Kingdom, his Church, and we are his people. We own nothing yet are given everything we need to accomplish his good work.

> **Kingdom builders don't build for earthly recognition but rather for eternal echoes.**

Continue to use the tools you have been given, the blueprints he has laid before you in his Word, and get to work. Don't wait for permits to use holy ground. Don't leave anything unfinished, be faithful to every detail, and be content when you aren't recognized as the architect. You weren't created to construct castles for people's entertainment. What you have been asked to build is for Kingdom advancement.

Remember that while you are building, you are defending. You know your assignment, you know your enemy, and you know your God.

I cannot tell you how often I have thought *When will it be my turn?* after years of watching my peers step into their callings. I was always the understudy in the musicals, always the best friend and never the lead character. It was a lot of almost but not yet. A ton of don't call us we'll call you. Then when someone did approach me, I was called the wrong name, but it was better than never being acknowledged.

> It might feel like a big game of hide-and-seek but God has never taken his eyes off you.

This is how so many of us feel, but rather than voice our disappointment with our reality we grow angry with rejection and wildly jealous of others. We say we're fine, but we're seething. Yet this place of hiddenness that feels like forgotten-ness is for a purpose; it will teach us humility if nothing else.

It's here in no-man's-land we find God, coming to the end of ourselves so he can finally get to work in us. While we're having pity parties and worrying about who is getting what, God has masterfully been preparing our steps for holy work. Good work.

It might feel like a big game of hide-and-seek but God has never taken his eyes off you.

If you're searching for the holy in your hiddenness, the reward in the unseen places, the glory in the gory details of pressing in when everyone else seems to be stepping out, know that God sees you in the secret places where sweat pours, and tears stream, and your hands are calloused from building something another will call their home.

It isn't easy being the worker when the world says success is owning the home. From your position on the scaffolding, you can see the enemy coming and what is on the horizon, and you are skilled with both the hammer and the sword. Stay in position: those standing in the shadows, those praying on the precipice, those fighting on the fringes. You aren't invisible, you are an intricate part of God's strategy. All of heaven is watching even if nobody around you seems to know who you are. Your name is on the lips of your Father and he knows exactly who you are and where you are.

Those looking for the Holy in the hidden, know you are standing on Holy ground. God isn't interested in your visibility as much as your availability.

A Rising Remnant

Just as the 120 gathered in the Upper Room were filled with the Holy Spirit as the Church was born, we, the remnant, are in position to receive from the Lord power and authority to take the message of Jesus Christ to not only a lost world but a hurting Church.

Perhaps the Church is one of the most lost people groups on planet earth right now, yet God is still breathing life over us and fanning his flame in us. He isn't finished with us yet. As we come together for corporate worship, spontaneous gatherings, meals around tables, as we contend for community and choose unity as his family, we will see his Kingdom come on earth as it is in heaven.

This rising remnant will be made up of unlikely servants who believe in God's promises and carry a deep love for God and his people. As the apostles continued their mission as documented in the book of Acts, they were confronted with challenges and opposition, yet they remained focused on their task at hand. It's the same for us today.

I know we've all been hurt, disappointed, and rejected. But I see you healing, gathering up the brokenness as God prepares to make a masterpiece out of the mess. I see you getting out of bed when you'd rather cover your head. I hear you praying a line or two, the lingering hope in your weary voice, when it has felt like God was silent. I'm watching you hug the necks of those who stabbed you in the back and speak life about those who nearly killed you; forgiveness is so becoming on you, wear it like a fine perfume.

Others see it too: the Great Healer doing a deep work in you and on you. Those scars aren't scary, they are holy. Wear them honestly. Bare them boldly.

This next great revival in God's Church won't come from those of us who have never been wounded, but rather will be led by those with bumps and lumps who have refused to give up. God sees you here too. Sowing seeds when you'd rather be buried, staying when you'd prefer to leave, and choosing reconciliation over revenge.

This healing journey for each of us, for our churches, is not for the faint of heart. You aren't alone; we're all being pieced back together and patched up as we build together. Rest when you can, but keep your eyes on the final product, the beautiful Bride of Christ.

Don't get distracted. Don't be discouraged. God does good work in our brokenness and makes his power known in our healing.

A House That Jesus Is Building

I leaned up against my kitchen wall, taking it all in. Grown cousins, shoeless in their Christmas socks and flannel pj's, lounging on the couches, sharing funny TikToks with each other from across the room, my parents and in-laws at the dining-room table sipping post-Christmas dessert coffee, our dog hopping room to room hoping someone would drop a leftover his way. My youngest was in the front room by the Christmas tree digging through her treasures, running to show us her newest toys, and we shared in her delight knowing she was our last to bask in all the Santa magic.

This house that just seven months ago had been nothing but dusty floorboards and exposed drywall on a chaotic construction site is now a home. It is my home, and it is filled with the people who I love. That is all I dreamed of in those early days of impatiently waiting for it to be complete.

Sure, there are some finishing touches that still need to be made. Is any house ever completely finished? We're always looking for ways to improve and polish even the newest spaces, but most importantly it's a safe place for those we love.

As I watched my sister help my youngest free Barbies from their packaging and my husband talk quietly with his oldest nephew (listening to the sounds of community), I thought of how this book began and how chaotic everything felt while building this house. I had been so worried about the tiniest of details and overwhelmed by what I couldn't control. Now here we are, each room overflowing with joy and being used with intentionality over food, good conversation, the generous sharing of gifts and kind words.

I see you too, churches.

You're beautiful.

This book was never intended to point fingers and make us feel guilty for our past mistakes and failures as leaders and those who represent our churches. I certainly don't have all the answers. We know we've built on the wrong foundations; after all, there are critics all around to remind us we haven't always gotten it right and yet we're still standing. We're staying because God is on the throne. We know which foundation we should be building on.

Just like Christmas morning in our new home that months before was just a frame, we are now stripped down to the simplicity of the Gospel with Jesus as our true foundation. We have an opportunity to fill a renewed, stronger church house with our precious church family.

A safe house.

A warm house.

The House that Jesus is building.

Final Thoughts

I want to see the Church in all her glory, the Bride of Christ radiant in these days of darkness and despair. I know God loves his Church far more than we do, and he doesn't need us to defend her. He is simply asking us to love her.

God has graciously invited us to partner with him in building something beautiful. Though we have the tools and resources at our fingertips, it is God and God alone who is the master builder. Thank you, God, for trusting us with your Church and your people. I want to leave you with this:

> So, my dear Christian friends, companions in following this call to the heights, take a good hard look at Jesus. He's the centerpiece of everything

we believe, faithful in everything God gave him to do. Moses was also faithful, but Jesus gets far more honor. A builder is more valuable than a building any day. Every house has a builder, but the Builder behind them all is God. Moses did a good job in God's house, but it was all servant work, getting things ready for what was to come. Christ as Son is in charge of the house. (Heb. 3:1–6 MSG)

Rise up, radical remnant.
For such a time as this.

ACKNOWLEDGMENTS

I couldn't do this without the love and support of my husband Tony and our two daughters who have cheered me on through late night edits and the frenzy of releasing a book. Thank you for praying for me, believing in the message God has given me and carrying it alongside me. You are my greatest joy and ministry and I love you so much.

To the church pastors and leaders who have invited me into your church home with open arms and a great hope for healing and revival, thank you for trusting me with your people and loving me and my family as your own. I cannot and will not do this without you, we are in this together, in it to finish it.

To my local church family and our pastors, thank you for pastoring us and providing a safe and healthy place for us to come and worship as a family in this season of ministry.

To my publishers David C Cook and the entire team who have believed in this message God has asked me to carry and release, thank you for championing me and carrying me when this felt heavy and unknown. I am honored to be one of you authors and to call you my friends.

And finally, thank you, Jesus. For your Church, your Word, your promises and your people. You are our firm foundation and it is an honor to build the Kingdom alongside you and together with my brothers and sisters in the faith. May we be your ready architects.

NOTES

1. A. W. Tozer, *Man: The Dwelling Place of God—What It Means to Have Christ Living in You* (Chicago: Moody, 2008), 11.

2. Brody Carter, "New Barna Survey Finds That 38 Percent of US Pastors Have Considered Leaving Ministry," CBN, November 16, 2021, www2.cbn.com/news /us/new-barna-survey-finds-38-us-pastors-have-considered-leaving-ministry.

3. Barna Group, "Signs of Decline and Hope among Key Metrics of Faith," March 4, 2020, www.barna.com/research/changing-state-of-the-church/.

4. C. S. Lewis, *The Lion, the Witch and the Wardrobe* (New York: Harper, 1978), 38–40.

5. Precept Austin, "Acts 2 Commentary," November 8, 2023, www.preceptaustin.org/acts-2-commentary#2:1.

6. L.A.M.B., "Jude 1; Contending for the Faith," Christianity Board, September 28, 2023, www.christianityboard.com/threads/jude1-contending-for-the -faith.58268/.

7. "No Longer Slaves," on Jonathan David Helser, Brian Mark Johnson, and Joel Case, *Peace*, Bethel Music, 2020.

8. "Dr. Martin Luther King Jr. Speech at Illinois Wesleyan University, 1966," Illinois Wesleyan University, accessed February 25, 2024, www.iwu.edu/mlk/page-4.html.

9. Merriam-Webster, s.v. "revival," accessed February 26, 2024, www.merriam-webster.com/dictionary/revival.

10. Ray Stedman, "Sermon Series—Expository Studies in Acts," Precept Austin, January 17, 2024, www.preceptaustin.org/acts_commentaries.

11. Merriam-Webster, s.v. "remnant," accessed February 26, 2024, www.merriam-webster.com/dictionary/remnant.

12. L. V. Meyer, s.v. "remnant," *The Anchor Yale Bible Dictionary*, ed. D. Freedman, et al. (New York: Doubleday, 1992), 669–71.

13. Merriam-Webster, "The Roots of 'Radical,'" accessed February 26, 2024, www.merriam-webster.com/wordplay/radical-word-history.

BIBLE CREDITS

The author has added italics, bold, and all capitals to Scripture quotations for emphasis.